# SOUTH AFRICAN DISPATCHES

# SOUTH AFRICAN DISPATCHES

## LETTERS TO MY COUNTRYMEN

DONALD WOODS

FOREWORD BY
ALAN PATON

An Owl Book

HENRY HOLT AND COMPANY
NEW YORK

FOR HAROLD LEVY

*Barrister and friend,*
*who twice kept me*
*out of prison*

Copyright © 1986 by Donald Woods

Published by Henry Holt and Company, Inc.,
115 West 18th Street, New York, New York 10011.
Published in Canada by Fitzhenry & Whiteside Limited,
195 Allstate Parkway, Markham, Ontario L3R 4T8.

Library of Congress Cataloging-in-Publication Data
Woods, Donald, 1933—
South African dispatches.
1. South Africa—Politics and government—1961–1978.
2. South Africa—Race relations.   3. Apartheid—South
Africa.   I. Title.
DT779.9.W66   1987   305.8'00968   86–11934
ISBN: 0-8050-0143-3
ISBN: 0-8050-0783-0 (An Owl book: pbk.)

First published in hardcover by Henry Holt and Company, Inc.,
in 1987.
First Owl Book Edition—1988

Designed by Katy Riegel
Printed in the United States of America
3  5  7  9  10  8  6  4  2


ISBN 0-8050-0783-0

# CONTENTS

v

# CONTENTS

# CONTENTS

# FOREWORD

by Alan Paton

This collation is a fine dish, bits of the prophet Amos served up with Rabelaisian sauce, with a strong taste of John Stuart Mill, and in the far background, old Socrates himself . . .

Donald Woods is scathing about pussyfoots, so I shall refrain from anything that smacks of sanctimony and shall not use the words *courageous, outspoken, invincible,* and my favorite phrase, "the indestructible human spirit." In any case, these articles are very much of the earth, earthy. Much more appropriate are words like *biting* and *irreverent.* I looked hard for traces of libertinism, communism, and antinomianism but couldn't find any—yet I wouldn't say it's the kind of book the minister of transport would like his daughter to see on the railway bookstall.

It is iconoclastic—it takes national demigods and knocks them off their perches. All this is done without malice. At least that's what I think, but it wasn't I who got knocked off the perch. This book doesn't show inordinate respect for those who rule our lives in South Africa.

It is, in short, a book in praise of freedom and in defense of freedom. It is in praise of that kind of freedom which is the right of every human being who is born upon this earth, a "freedom to do what he likes within reasonable laws." It is the kind of freedom that must not interfere with the freedom of my neighbor to do what *he* likes within reasonable laws. Such a book must also praise and defend the rule of law, which is the most noble concept of sinful man, and this it does.

In our country the rule of law has to such a great and dangerous extent been eroded that the freedom the Voortrekkers sought has virtually disappeared from the lives of their children, many of whom do not know it. It is bad enough to live in a country where parliament gives away its own sovereignty to individual ministers, so that the right to deprive a man of his physical freedom is no longer the sole prerogative of the courts. But many of the children of the Voortrekkers are not aware of any threat to freedom, because it is their own ministers who now control it. That is the evil of Afrikaner

Nationalism, that so long as it thinks itself to be free it does not much concern itself about the freedom of others.

One cannot be a defender of freedom in South Africa unless one is an opponent of Afrikaner Nationalism. Donald Woods is unequivocally so. It cannot be otherwise. Therefore he brings down wrath on his head, for while Afrikaner Nationalism thinks it can do without friends, it hates its enemies, especially those who live in its own country. Woods knows this, and accepts it as the price one must pay to be a defender of freedom. "Here I stand, I can do no other."

These articles are all good, but some of them are gems. "Meet Fighting Father Mac" is a masterpiece. Obviously Woods likes Mac because Mac is also a mixture of Amos and Rabelais. The closing story is inimitable. "Pussyfoots in the Pulpit" and its successor, "High Priests of Outrage," are also masterpieces; what Woods says is clear and painful when he writes that "the sheer skill with which they [the preachers] avoid the major moral issue of our time and place is remarkable."

In the piece "Bogeymen Ride into Bryanston," Woods lambastes the United Party and its twenty-seven years of double-talk, quoting the party leader, De Villiers Graaff, as saying that "the United Party is a party of radical conservatism." Says Woods: "Radical conservatism indeed! Liberal totalitarianism. Democratic dictatorship. Communist capitalism. Sick health. Dry wet. Gobbledegookityzookaboowoopazang." Nice comment.

I shall close with a few words about one piece that

shows that Donald Woods is not a bad writer. It is different, too, because it gets away from the tumult and the heartbreak of our politics. It is called "Where Time Stands Still," and it is about the small village of Rhodes on the mountain roof of South Africa, on that magnificent road that runs from Maclear to Mohales Hoek, over Naude's Nek, one of the highest road passes in Africa, and through places with names like Wartrail, Moshesh's Ford, Lundean's Nek. There's no Amos, no Rabelais, no John Stuart Mill here, only the great mountains and the great valleys and Meneer Buytendag who looks after everything. There's nothing to do in the evenings, and an old patriarch and his five sons once sat in the far past, round the sitkamer smoking and saying nothing. Well, almost nothing beyond that inimitable Afrikaans expression ja-nee (yes-no), which means ho-hum. Every now and then the old man would take his pipe out of his mouth, sigh deeply, and say: "Ja, nee . . . " Whereupon one of the sons would respectfully respond "Ja, Pa!"

Well, Donald Woods, people are going to ask each other if your book is any good. Some, especially the dispersched, are going to say: "Nee!" Others, the pussyfoots, will say: "Ja, nee . . . " But many, including me, are going to say: "Ja!"

*Alan Paton*
*Durban, Natal*
*South Africa, 1977*

# INTRODUCTION

Donald Woods had been editor of the *Daily Dispatch* in South Africa, and author of its most widely syndicated newspaper column, for twelve years when he was arrested and banned for accusing the South African government of responsibility for the death of his friend, the black leader Steve Biko. This book is a selection of his columns from 1975 until his arrest and subsequent banning in late 1977, reflecting the political atmosphere in the country at that time, from the point of view of a white journalist whose criticisms of the apartheid policy grew markedly more severe up to the time of Biko's death.

Originally assembled for book publication in South Africa a decade ago, the manuscript was put aside when the banning order intervened. Three months after his arrest, Woods, disguised as a Catholic priest, and his family, traveling separately, escaped from South Africa to Lesotho, then together by plane to Botswana, Zambia, and ultimately to Britain, where they have lived since January 1978 and where he now works as a writer, broadcaster, and lecturer on the apartheid issue.

*South African Dispatches* is a chronological record of the style and extent of one journalist's dissent as tolerated under South Africa's complex publication laws during a period that sparked the country's present crisis. Since then, several more laws have been added to limit reportage and comment on racial confrontation in South Africa.

Each of the pieces published in this collection was written to stay within the publication laws and regulations operative in South Africa at that time, because in spite of attempts to charge the writer with having contravened these regulations, the South African authorities were unable to secure a conviction in any court of law. Ultimately they resorted to extralegal methods to silence him, imposing a ban by cabinet decree that could not be challenged in court.

The title *South African Dispatches* was selected because the articles were written in South Africa and were dispatches in the full sense of the word—messages to compatriots. The title is also a tribute to the *Daily Dispatch*, which for more than a century was noted for its opposition to racial extremism under various administrations in South Africa. It was an unusual newspaper in several respects. Commercially profitable, it was controlled entirely by staff members through a trust that dispensed two-thirds of all dividends to charities. Only staff members and their families were shareholders, and all seven directors on the board were executives of the newspaper, including the editor and his deputy.

During the author's editorship more than half the newspaper's readers were blacks, but after his arrest and banning the paper adopted a more conservative policy.

Donald Woods comments: "Rereading these pieces ten years after they were written—with only slight editing to make references understandable to a non–South African readership—brings back clearly to me the atmosphere in South Africa at a time, as hindsight now shows, when the crude rope with which the Afrikaner Nationalist Party government held bound its citizens was beginning to unravel. The editors of provincial newspapers showed considerable courage in publishing my column, especially in the city of Bloemfontein, where government supporters threatened violence because of the column's continued publication. Ironically, the decision by *The Friend* of Bloemfontein to discontinue it because of local anger came in the very week that I was banned, making that editorial decision unnecessary. Nonetheless, tribute is deserved for the years of government anger that were defied by this and other newspapers.

"In my case the government tolerated considerable criticism—until certain points were raised about the Biko killing, which when quoted in overseas newspapers caused severe embarrassment to South African embassies and consulates abroad. That was the crunch point, hence the ban.

"As for the ban itself, I have regarded it as an undeserved honor that has been of immense help in my work, and when it was reimposed after five years to maintain the prohibition against my being quoted inside South Africa I was reassured that my years in exile were not being wasted."

—*The Publisher*

# SOUTH AFRICAN DISPATCHES

# BEHIND THE
# VORSTER MASK

*Balthazar Johannes Vorster, prime minister of South Africa from 1966 to 1978, was the subject of the opening column in January 1975. A forbidding figure who introduced imprisonment without trial for political dissidents, he was forever threatening to crack down on the country's handful of antiapartheid newspapers and to add to the twenty-two statutes that limited what could be published in the press.*

There is a difference between the public image and the private personality of Prime Minister Vorster. His public image is that of the grim Volksleader, with downturned lips, devoid of all sense of levity. But those who know him maintain that he has been seen to smile.

They say he has to be quite considerably amused or intrigued for this to happen. Which prompts the intriguing question—what intrigues Mr. Vorster? What does he do in his leisure moments? Has he a hobby?

One of his special interests is chess. In fact, he is **a**

I

chess fanatic, with a variety of sets made of various substances—glass, steel, silver, and wood, as well as the regulation plastic. He learned the game in detention camp during World War II, when General Jan Smuts imprisoned him for subversive activities on the wrong side of that conflict.

Premier Vorster talks readily about those days and his reliance on what he calls "rock post"—sympathizers used to get the news to him and his fellow prisoners by wrapping news bulletins around rocks and lobbing them over the wire into the compound. He came to depend on this primitive form of selective news truncation.

Maybe that's why he now feels a proper press is unnecessary.

When he was arrested his wife wasn't allowed to tell the rest of the family where he was being held (in the Port Elizabeth police cells), so she sent a telegram reading: "John is staying at the King's Hotel," and they got the message.

The young Vorster went on a hunger strike in protest, to further a cause directly opposed to national policy as determined by majority vote of the South African parliament. His conversion to constitutionality and his zeal to limit all protest to the ballot box came only later in life when, by happy coincidence, the key to that same ballot box was in his capacious pocket.

Where once he endured punishment without trial for his ideals, being branded as subversive for challenging the government of the day, now he is the one doing the branding, and today's challengers are on the receiving end. How the pendulum does swing, and is likely to keep swinging. . . .

And although his interest in chess isn't as bizarre as the fact that his political heir apparent, Interior Minister C. P. Mulder, wrote his academic thesis on hopscotch, there is some significance in the Vorster chess syndrome, because today Mr. Vorster is engaged in his biggest-ever chess game.

He has drawn the white pieces and therefore has the opening initiative, but as every chess buff knows it is black's response that shapes the end game. And in this particular chess game there are five times more black pieces than white ones.

# MINISTER MULDER'S HOPSCOTCH THESIS

*Dr. C. P. Mulder, minister of the interior, was Vorster's political heir apparent and the second most powerful man in the government. His party projected him as a personage of dignity and intellectual eminence, and the discovery that his academic thesis had been about the game of hopscotch was something of a scoop. One of his main rivals was Dr. P. G. Koornhof, minister of sport, who constantly sought ways of gaining readmission for South African teams into international sport following the worldwide boycott over apartheid.*

The reference in this column to Interior Minister Mulder's thesis on hopscotch has attracted considerable interest, and I have acquired a microfilm copy of it on the assurance that reproduction of it does not imperil state security.

Entitled "Hopscotch, or Hinkspel, a Description of the Game as it Appears in South Africa," the thesis is a scholarly work that begins by probing the origins of hopscotch. Dr. Mulder assures us that it was played by children in ancient Greece, and that Pliny mentions the game. There were also references to it in the Middle

Ages and some authorities (hopscologists?) detect traces of demonology in some of the early terms.

The interior minister concentrates most of his research on South African manifestations of the game, which is no less than we would expect from so patriotic a man, and he lists regional varieties from Calvinia to Potchefstroom.

But why did the minister choose hopscotch for his researches? Why didn't he choose Bok Bok, that far more interesting game in which schoolboys crash down onto each other's backs? Bok Bok would surely have been a more appropriate reflection of our national character and therefore an even more patriotic choice.

Consider the finer points of Bok Bok. There has to be someone to jump on and the object of the game is for the jumper to seek a superior position and therefore a privileged status. The essence of Bok Bok is not merely to improve one's own position, but to do so at discomfort to someone else, and it could be lent a higher tone by describing it as Maintaining Our Own Identity, or Preserving Our Traditional Way of Life.

A further refinement is that in Bok Bok, as in Maintaining Our Own Identity, you need not adhere to any absolute standard. You change the rules to suit yourself, then claim moral justification in terms of these changed rules. Here indeed lies a rich field for South African research.

So it is a pity that Interior Minister Mulder hopped so impetuously into research on a less national game. But Sports Minister Koornhof could remedy the oversight by restoring Bok Bok to its rightful place in our national sport. And as we call our national sportsmen Springboks, or Boks for short, he might contemplate allowing nonracial Bok Bok at club level, among consenting adults in private.

Then we might be allowed back into international sport, and a Bok Bok representative for South Africa could be called a Bok Bok Bok.

# THE LAST CAUCASIAN CAUCUS

*The governing Afrikaner Nationalist Party came to power in 1948, replacing the more moderate but still segregationist United Party of General Jan Smuts. At the time of this article, February 1975, the leader of the United Party was Sir De Villiers Graaff, who was noted for his indecisiveness in matters of political policy. The Progressive Party opposed apartheid but had few members in the South African parliament.*

Consider our national parliament in Cape Town—the world's last Caucasian Caucus. What a mountain of racial legislation has been enacted in this assembly reserved for Caucasoids only.

Last week I was a lunch guest there of Progressive Party leader Colin Eglin, whose victory in the Sea Point by-election was certain from the moment Piet Cillie, editor of *Die Burger*, predicted otherwise. If Cillie predicts anything you may be sure the opposite will happen.

The parliamentary dining room is historic. In the last

century it was the debating chamber of the Cape parliament, when members were elected by voters of all races under a qualified franchise. This was, of course, before the idea of a nonracial system was regarded as "before its time."

Once in this room I met the veteran Smutsite MP, Dr. Douglas Smit, who was very deaf and spoke in a booming voice. Within a few feet of the first apartheid cabinet, who were taking their collective lunch at an adjoining table, Dr. Smit leaned over to me confidentially to shout: "They're a thoroughly bad lot. Smuts should have hanged them for treason."

The "thoroughly bad lot" were new to power in those days, and apart from an angry reddening of ears there was no reaction to the observation. Dr. Smit's deafness was legendary. Once he took some journalists for coffee in the parliamentary dining room, and when the waiter told him what was owing he gave him half the amount. The waiter stared at the inadequate money and pointed out that he hadn't been paid enough. Dr. Smit looked up at him and beamed benignly. "Don't worry about the change," he said.

The waiter retired in some confusion, then returned to pluck at the doctor's sleeve, extending the money to explain the deficiency, but Dr. Smit waved him away with a reassuring laugh, booming: "No, no, my lad. The rest is for YOU. That is your TIP."

The waiter gave up the unequal struggle, and one of the journalists later sought him out to redress the inequity.

The eating habits of politicians are revealing. Prime Minister Vorster surveys his plate somberly before selecting any morsel, as if searching for Communists under the lettuce. If United Party leader Graaff is confronted with three morsels he chooses the middle one, then appears to doubt his choice.

Talking of food and politicians, I was a houseguest of Dr. Zac de Beer in Lusaka recently, where he presides over the Oppenheimer copper mining interests in Zambia, and as we had to get up early for a flight to Ndola, breakfast was served at an ungodly hour. There, confronting me on the breakfast plate, were two completely white eggs. White yolks and all. Dr. de Beer, who always expresses himself precisely, said: "There is a nutritional deficiency in Zambian hens, hence the white yolks, but it affects only their coloration, and you will find they are not unpalatable."

Strange, though, isn't it, to have all-white eggs in Zambia?

Almost as strange as having an all-white parliament in South Africa.

# I ARRANGED
# A BOGUS
# MARRIAGE

*Under South Africa's influx control laws every black person living and working in a white-zoned urban area had to be "registered"—given state permission to be there. This was recorded in a passport-type reference book, known as a "pass," which contained comprehensive information about the person, including fingerprints and personal details.*

I arranged a bogus marriage recently, followed by a bogus divorce, but both the marriage and the divorce were entirely legal.

I had returned home from the office to find my children's nursemaid, Dolly Radebe, being arrested as an unregistered black person. The men in uniform explained that because her mother in the urban township had died, Dolly could no longer legally remain in the urban area and would have to go to the Transkei "homeland" where she had been born.

I protested that she had no relatives there, knew nobody there, would be unemployed and destitute there, and was too young to fend for herself. They said the law had to be obeyed and she would be imprisoned if she didn't leave the area within seventy-two hours.

A township expert on the subject of influx control laws and the pass regulations revealed that there was one way to foil the system. An unregistered black female can become a registered black female if she becomes legally married to a registered black male.

So a wedding was arranged.

Finding a cooperative minister of religion from the township was no problem, and for a suitable consideration we also found a compliant bridegroom who could be relied on not to take the marriage vows too literally. It was a lovely ceremony.

On the Monday morning Dolly produced her marriage certificate and was duly registered by one of the officials who had been ready to authorize her arrest. He didn't even recognize her. You know how all blacks look alike to some people.

So on the Tuesday when the men in uniform arrived to take her away, we produced Dolly's registration stamp in her passbook, declining to enlighten the puzzled officials as to how her illegality had so quickly been transformed into legality.

After a decent interval my township expert arranged a convenient divorce for Dolly, but her registration remained indelibly in her passbook. She was legal. She was a Registered Black Person. And today, some months later, she is happily and genuinely married ("remarried," to be legally precise) so her registration and legality are doubly assured.

And now that the officials concerned will discover through this article how her original legality was attained, it is important to give the assurance that all was correctly done to comply with the regulations.

And while I freely admit that I arranged a marriage that was phoney and a divorce that was phoney, I would be deeply hurt if anyone suggested that the marriage and divorce in question were illegal.

Illegal? You won't easily catch me doing anything illegal.

Hell, nobody respects the law more than I do.

# TWO MEN
# IN A BATHROOM

*Any black person could be stopped at any time by the police and told to produce a "pass," and if unable to do so could be arrested and imprisoned. In spite of this law, under which about 200,000 blacks per year were imprisoned, blacks without "passes" were frequently found seeking work in white suburbs as gardeners or domestic workers.*

Last week's account of how to arrange a bogus marriage to circumvent influx control regulations appears to have been received with interest, but there are even more bizarre ways of cheating the pass laws.

Some months ago I arrived home to find a police van outside my house, and some stalwarts in uniform about to enter the front door in pursuit of two blacks they believed to be unregistered. They had challenged the two to produce their passes to prove they were allowed to be in a white area, and the two had run away.

"We saw them run this way, and we think they're in your house," said the chief stalwart. I told them to watch the front door while I looked inside, and they appeared to appreciate such cooperation, perceiving it would make easier their task of Preserving Our Own Identity and Protecting Our Traditional Way of Life.

Inside the house I ran upstairs to be told by my wife that she had hidden the two men in the guest room. After a hasty consultation she took the two men into a bathroom with her and locked the door, knowing it would be beyond the parameters of a white South African policeman's mentality to conceive of a white woman being locked in a bathroom with two black men.

Meanwhile the men in uniform were admitted to begin their search, which was painstakingly thorough. They looked everywhere—under beds, in cupboards, behind curtains. I couldn't resist standing guiltily in front of one cupboard I knew to be completely empty, so naturally they wanted to look inside. No need, I said, the cupboard was empty, and I stayed in front of it moving my eyes furtively from side to side in what I hoped was a guilty manner. They ordered me to step aside (ve haff vays) and it was a pleasant moment when they opened the door and went through the whole Mother Hubbard bit.

I think it was that empty cupboard that broke them, because their search became increasingly listless thereafter.

Finally I indicated the bathroom door, and the chief

stalwart seized the handle just as my wife, with perfect timing, announced her occupancy. They backed away as if stung, apologizing to her through the locked door.

After they left, the two fugitives emerged falling about with laughter at the whole episode, and when the coast was clear and they could go on their way, the two were still chuckling.

Such a sense of humor the black people have.
So far.

# THE MYSTICAL
# CALL OF
# KOFFIEFONTEIN

*Koffiefontein is a small village in South Africa's central province of Orange Free State, which was named in honor of the Dutch royal family in the last century—the House of Orange. Although the eastern part of the province is scenically attractive, the western part in which Koffiefontein is located is notoriously dry and flat. The village's sole claim to distinction is that pro-Axis subversives were interned there during World War II.*

How's this for the quote of the week, from pilot Welgemoed on flight 409 out of Kimberley: "On the right-hand side of the aircraft you can see Koffiefontein." What was the significance of this announcement? Who on earth would want, in the ordinary course of things, to see Koffiefontein? What particular Koffiefontein quality merited the craning of passengers' necks for special observation of this blighted desert spot in the middle of nowhere?

(Nowhere being, of course, the Orange Free State.)

Perhaps pilot Welgemoed is a dedicated member of

the governing Afrikaner Nationalist Party and felt we
should all look with reverence on Koffiefontein because
that was where Prime Minister Vorster was interned
during World War II for sympathizing too zealously with
Der Führer.

Yet no compound was visible from the air at that distance, nor was anything else to distinguish the sun-
baked hamlet. The pilot could not have been calling our
attention to any scenic attraction because Koffiefontein
looked, on that arid plain, like some Algerian redoubt
from Beau Geste, and one could imagine legionnaires
reeling around in the heat as dozing camels blinked
their bleary eyes.

Perhaps we were simply too far away to see the best
features of the place. There in the distance, for example,
was a darkish patch. Was it a dam? This conjured up
all sorts of Arthurian possibilities, like an arm rising
from the depths clothed in white samite, mystic, won-
derful, brandishing a Boer rifle three times before sink-
ing again among the tadpoles.

Why shouldn't such an Excalibur-type myth be part
of the legends of our Volk? Most of our myths are far
less probable, and there have been others almost as po-
etic, like the old prophesy from Afrikaner lore long ago
that a man from the Cape dressed all in brown would
arise to unite the people. For some years Opposition
leader Graaff took to dressing in all brown before finally
abandoning hope and returning to Tygerberg worsted.
He does, however, retain that rather agricultural brown
hat of his.

Premier Vorster also affects a headpiece of rural character, though it is more solemn than Graaff's. It is a grim hat, a determined hat. The very downturn of the brim bespeaks the solemn Volksleader image so persistently sought by He Who Defends Our Traditional Way of Life, even when he is playing golf.

Golf! Maybe that's it! Maybe Koffiefontein was where Prime Minister Vorster was first drawn to relieve the boredom of incarceration by taking up golf, and maybe the arm that rose from the limpid waters of the dam was brandishing a number seven iron rather than a Boer rifle.

Perhaps, indeed, there exists in that blighted spot of Koffiefontein some sacred soil upon which Mr. Vorster once practiced his chipping. Perhaps it was there that, urged on by some weatherbeaten veteran of the OssewaBrandwag or the Blackshirts or the Greyshirts or the Stormjaers, he worked on his bunker shots or used the Arthurian dam as a water hazard—when if he topped the ball the arm would rise from the waters to save it, because it, the ball, was white.

An arm clothed, of course, in white samite.

Mystic. Wonderlik.

# MEET FIGHTING
# FATHER MAC

*A kudu is a large antelope whose hunting is strictly prohibited by law in the nature reserve of Addo, Eastern Cape Province. The Catholic Church in South Africa is not indigenously broad-based, hence most Catholic priests in the country are from abroad—especially from Germany, Switzerland, and Ireland.*

The small Cape Province village of Komga is noted for its butter and antiques, and also its unusual parish priest. Father Matthew McManus, recently retired, was exiled to this remote spot by his bishop for poaching kudu buck in the Addo Forest near Port Elizabeth. Before he was fined, the magistrate asked if he had anything to say and he replied: "Yes, your honor, this is a case of much kudu about nothing." Fellow priests believe it was more for the pun than the poaching that the bishop expelled him to the edge of the diocese.

Born in Kilkenny, Ireland, Father McManus has spent most of his life in South Africa. Now in his late sixties, he looks like a bigger version of Spencer Tracy, with a shock of silver hair and a jaw that juts out aggressively. A former boxing instructor, all he ever wanted to be was a simple parish priest—but he kept getting into trouble.

The first time he incurred the wrath of his bishop was for beating up three men one night at a hot-dog stand in Port Elizabeth. According to an eyewitness, Father McManus was quietly sipping coffee when the aggressive young men started picking on him, and when one of them hooked a finger into his priest's collar he knocked out the nearest two and was seen pursuing the third into the night, kicking at him as he ran.

Dispatched to a rural mission as a form of punishment, he became a versatile cleric. He learned to pilot a plane, stitch a wound, and deliver babies, also to be a master carpenter and radio technician. He once rigged up a fake radio broadcast for Father Michael Ahearne of Grahamstown, a homesick fellow Irishman who wanted an "international receiving set" so that he could listen to broadcasts from Dublin.

With the help of a stooge, one Father O'Brien of the same parish, Father McManus stood a cheap local radio on a windowsill, placed microphones behind it, and with the aid of a tape recorder operated by Father O'Brien "switched on" so that Father Ahearne could try out the set before buying it. First the "news" came over in Gaelic, then there was a violin jig, an Irish song, and a brief report about a hurling match. Father Ahearne was so delighted that he paid thirty rands for the radio and took it away with him back to Grahamstown.

Confronted with this story Father McManus literally wept with laughter as he added: "Ahearne sat up for three nights trying to get Dublin, and all the poor bugger got was Grahamstown."

After a while he was reprieved from rural duty and given a probationary parish in Cradock, until the bishop heard of how he was dealing with wife beaters—he was beating them up. The women of the town approved, but complaints from the men eventually spread to Port Elizabeth. One of the complainants was a minister of the Dutch Reformed Church whose deacon had been on the receiving end of the McManus ministry after his desperate wife had taken the unusual step of appealing beyond the limits of Calvinism for assistance.

Now given a spell in one of the toughest black townships adjoining Port Elizabeth, where Friday night stabbings and assaults were so commonplace that even the police stayed away, McManus became a popular vigilante. He used to patrol the township at night armed only with a club and come out with a collection of confiscated knives. The residents still tell of how he used to stitch up stab wounds on the spot with ordinary cotton, pushing in the needle with a coin.

Then an epidemic of bubonic plague raged through the township, and he was the only volunteer prepared to enter the stricken area to tend the sick and bury the dead. He moved in and lived there throughout the epidemic and only ventured out to find new plague victims and bring them in for nursing. Hundreds were dying, and there was so little help that he carried most of the patients in on his own broad back.

He never caught the disease, but his courage made such an impression on all at the time that he was presented with an illuminated scroll by the Port Elizabeth municipality and the blacks renamed one of their township streets after him.

Posted to a white parish again, he was soon in trouble. A delegation of leading parishioners called at the sacristy while he was donning his vestments for Mass, to complain against blacks being allowed to come up to the communion rail at the same time as whites. It wasn't his rejection of their complaint that caused the bishop anguish, it was the manner of it. The bishop felt it hadn't been necessary to throw them physically out of the sacristy while shouting: "Get stuffed, ye bastards!"

Removed to another parish nearer the edge of the diocese, Father McManus was reprimanded for suborning a number of priests from neighboring parishes into his notorious poker school, which often was an all-night affair featuring whisky and violent argument. Then came the first of several kudu-poaching incidents, culminating in his conviction and fine.

This resulted in his ultimate exile to Komga, the last parish in the diocese with the Kei River as its boundary. When I visited Father McManus there he observed: "Sure, if His Lordship could have sent me across the river he would have done so." But he had some comfort in his exile. Pope John XXIII heard of the "wild priest" from South Africa while Father McManus was on a pilgrimage to Rome and sent for him. He knelt before the Pope for his blessing, but the Pope yanked him up by the ears and embraced him, calling him "my Matthew" and thanking him for his work during the township plague. I asked Father Mac if the Pope had been critical of his behavior in any way. "Ah, not at all," he said. "Thanks be to Jesus he obviously hadn't heard about that bloody kudu."

Now that Fighting Father Mac is retired back in Ireland and beyond the reach of his bishop, I can disclose something that happened on the eve of his retirement. The facts come from his old friend Father John McVeagh.

Simple country priests don't get much money for the small pleasures of life, so it took Father McManus and Father McVeagh two full years of diligent poker playing to get together enough money for a treat these two old priests had long craved—a cruise along the coast from Durban to Cape Town.

The cruise ship had barely left Durban before they sneaked from the tourist-class up into the first-class lounge to have a drink in style, but the more they tried to catch the eye of the pompous headwaiter to order a drink, the more he preferred to notice the wealthy American and British tourists, who seemed better prospects for generous tipping than the two impecunious-looking old clergymen.

He walked past them several times to take orders from other passengers, as Father McVeagh lamented: "The fella's ignorin' us, Mac, and me dying of the thirst." Father Mac's eyes glinted ominously. "I'll fix him," he said.

After several more attempts he managed to catch the headwaiter's eye, and the latter reluctantly walked over to stand before them. Father McManus said nothing, but on his face was the look of a shy, gentle old priest as he diffidently beckoned the headwaiter closer.

The headwaiter finally realized that the kindly old clergyman wanted to say something confidential, so he bent his ear down attentively.

And into his ear Father McManus said quietly but distinctly:

"Fuck off."

# MARTIANS IN THE LANGKLOOF?

*For whatever reason, whether atmospheric or escapist, South Africans are constantly reporting sightings of strange objects and lights in the sky, and it is wholly typical of the country's rulers to regard such reports as political matters falling within the jurisdiction of the security police.*

This week there have been more reports of strange objects in the South African skies. The latest comes from Joubertina, in the Langkloof district of Cape Province, a small village consisting of a few dirt roads with houses along them and a little hotel—not the sort of place you would expect Martians to select for a landing site. The good burghers of Joubertina say they have seen strange lights in the sky and that a huge iron ball weighing a ton has suddenly appeared on the nearby farm of Kransfontein.

These goings-on in the Langkloof have prompted the

security police to move in, so we may confidently expect the whole thing to be bungled or ascribed to communism.

They have interviewed a local schoolteacher, Mr. A. J. Van Niekerk, who says the iron ball landed on and pulverized a large rock. Another man claims to have seen smoke coming from the iron ball and there is some talk around the town that the ball exerts a strange magnetic effect that draws people's eyes closer together.

The security police have now taken the iron ball away to Oudtshoorn, presumably for interrogation, so if you see any security police officer walking around with a pronounced squint, he's probably been on duty in the Langkloof.

Different communities react differently to such manifestations. Recently the people of Fort Beaufort reported sightings of a flying saucer, but they didn't bother to call in the security police. They left it all to an enterprising police constable, who opened fire on the thing with his revolver—and it hasn't been back to Fort Beaufort since. The sturdy folk of Fort Beaufort don't mess around with flying saucers. They attack.

Well, I'm not convinced they saw a flying saucer, or that an iron ball is causing a lot of eyes to cross in the Oudtshoorn interrogation cells right now, and I'm well aware these things can usually be explained. But I wasn't too skeptical about the Joubertina reports—until I read that the security police were involved.

Now I am totally skeptical, because where the security police are involved I don't believe a damn thing.

# AFRIKAANS BEGAN
# IN INDIA

*Of all the articles collected in this volume, none
aroused more anger and bomb threats than this one.
To suggest that the linguistic symbol of white Afrikaner Nationalism, the Afrikaans language, had its
origins in a black country was regarded as outra-
geously provocative.*

The Afrikaans language is
now being celebrated in festivals all over South Africa,
culminating in a final festival at the Afrikaans Language Monument near Paarl. This must be the only
monument in the world erected specifically to salute a
language, but whether or not one agrees with the idea
of monuments to languages, Afrikaans does deserve rec-
ognition for being the newest language in the world.

Once sneered at by superior English-speaking South
Africans as a kitchen dialect derived from low Dutch,
it has in fact as pure and legitimate a linguistic lineage

as Dutch or German and is nowhere near as bastardized as English in its lexicon.

The basic origins of Afrikaans can be traced to India, as can those of most European languages. Of all the Indo-European language groups, the direct ancestor of Afrikaans is the Indo-Germanic group later fragmented into German, Dutch, and Flemish.

Early in the Christian era the speakers of the Indo-European dialect called Proto-Germanic inhabited northern Europe. Tacitus, writing in 98 A.D., described them as a tribal society living in scattered settlements in wooded and marshy country. As they expanded throughout northern Europe, differences in dialect grew marked with the passing of the centuries, evolving into three main branches called West Germanic, East Germanic, and North Germanic.

From North Germanic came the Scandinavian languages; from East Germanic the Gothic languages, which died out in the seventeenth century; and from West Germanic came Franconian and Anglo-Frisian. From Franconian came Dutch and Flemish, and from Anglo-Frisian came English. From Dutch and Flemish came Afrikaans, the adaptation over two hundred years of the original Dutch spoken in 1652 by the settlers who came from southern Holland and what is today northern Belgium.

As the Dutch settlers lost touch over several generations with the culture of Holland and were joined by settlers from Germany and France, on the African veld they evolved their own language, which developed a practical vigor of its own. Those early pioneers had little use for the drawing-room niceties of Amsterdam. . . .

Today Afrikaans is more similar to Flemish than to Dutch, and when speaking it in Belgium, one is frequently asked where one learned Flemish. Once in a bar I heard a Belgian family speaking what I thought at first was Afrikaans, and when we had chatted for a while they were astonished to hear about this African language so like their own. An Irishman present later pointed me out to a friend and said: "Only two beers he had, and Jaysus didn't he get the gift o' tongues!"

The old sneer that Afrikaans gets you no further than the Cape Town dock gates is invalid. In fact in various parts of the world a knowledge of Afrikaans is more useful than a knowledge of English, enabling one to follow conversations, signs, and newspaper reports in such countries as Germany, Austria, Switzerland, Holland, Belgium, Norway, Sweden, and Denmark.

So as a language its qualities are undoubted. But it has an image problem among most South Africans. Millions of blacks regard it as the language of oppression, the language of apartheid, and this is conveyed in the pejorative term "isi-Bhulu" (the Boer language).

It is this image that must be changed if Afrikaans is to have the future development it deserves in South Africa, and there must also be a fundamental attitudinal change among most who speak it. Too many of them give the impression that although they are of Africa they won't face up to the fact and are obsessed with creating here a small European enclave.

People obsessed with whiteness of skin don't really belong in Africa. They should emigrate to northern Europe, where skin tends to be very white indeed. Their departure would leave the field to those really committed to South Africa as an African country, and to Afrikaans as an African language accepted by all here.

And if those obsessed with whiteness can't bear the thought of northern Europe, they should head south to Antarctica.

Down there practically everything is white.

# THE
# WERY WERSATILE
# OWAMBO

*Although Namibia is about twice the size of Texas, it has barely a million inhabitants, of whom most are Ovambo. The Herero lost most of their people in wars against colonial troops of imperial Germany before World War I, in which South Africa took the territory from the Germans and has held it ever since in defiance of United Nations resolutions.*

Why do government spokesmen call the Ovambo people the Owambo?

The Ovambo are the majority group in Namibia and because of their numerical strength they are the key element politically. Yet in spite of their importance our cabinet ministers and governmental media minions keep referring to them as the Owambo. . . .

They also have this strange habit of referring to Swapo (South West Africa Peoples' Organization) as "Swapu." But then precision is not a quality of language for which our rulers are noted. The other day a member of the

cabinet actually referred to South Africa as a democratic country.

This week in Windhoek the government is sponsor-
ing a conference of various groups—with the notable
exception of the "Owambo," not to mention "Swapu"—
to discuss the future of Namibia, and they are pinning
their hopes on a man they once hunted. He is the Herero leader, Chief Clemens Kapuuo, who these days is
considered so moderate that he actually gets mentioned
occasionally in bulletins of the South African Broadcasting Corporation.

It wasn't always so. I remember fleeing with him once
from the Windhoek security police to a meeting in a
dry Namibian gulch. I was a young reporter instructed
by my editor to find and interview dissidents, and after
ten days of frustrating search in Windhoek, Swakop-
mund, and other areas hadn't managed to track down a
single Swapo supporter. Local whites were very amused.
They kept assuring me there was no such thing as
Swapo really. It was largely a figment of the imagination of the United Nations and our English-language
press in South Africa.

Reflecting on this as I rode up in the hotel elevator, I
said to the uniformed Ovambo attendant: "Where the
hell is Swapo?" I spoke rhetorically, not expecting a
reply, and his response was a dull expression of incom-
prehension as if I had said: "Differential calculus is the
opiate of the masses."

But that elevator operator must have been a wery
wersatile Owambo, because shortly after I entered my

room another member of the hotel staff came in with a broom and started sweeping the floor. "You want to meet Swapo?" he said, and after checking my press credentials he directed me to go back to the elevator in ten minutes.

There I went, whereupon the same dull-looking "Owambo" took me down to the hotel basement and, to cut a long story short, to a full-scale Swapo meeting complete with chairman and secretary and some fifty members of the hotel staff. Shortly after this meeting I was driven by Chief Kapuuo out to a dry riverbed some twenty miles outside Windhoek—he "lost" our security police pursuer in the biggest cloud of cross-country dust I've ever seen—where waited the venerable Herero paramount, Hosea Kotako.

The scene was straight out of Salvador Dali. In the dry riverbed were three dining-room chairs, one for me, one for Kapuuo, and one for the ninety-two-year-old Kotako, who wore a suit and waistcoat and watch chain; his councillors sat around on the banks as we spoke.

That night at the hotel in Windhoek my table companions were kidding me again as sparkling wine was poured and a string orchestra played a selection of Viennese waltzes. It was while one of them was repeating his assurance as he held out his glass for a refill, that there was no such thing as Swapo, that I noticed that the waiter pouring his wine was the man who had chaired the meeting in the hotel basement earlier that afternoon.

Since then fourteen years have elapsed, Kotako has

died and Kapuuo is out of favor with Swapo—but the question that stays in my mind is this: If resistance in Namibia was that organized at a time whites didn't even know of its existence, how much more organized and widespread must it be now that the whole world knows of it?

Never underestimate the wery wersatile Owambo. . . .

# MANDELA SHOULD
# BE FREED

*Nelson Mandela, South Africa's most renowned African nationalist leader, was imprisoned in 1962, and at the time this article was written most white South Africans regarded it as practically treasonous to suggest his release.*

A white man, Ronald Cohen, has been freed five years after being convicted of murdering his wife.

A black man, Nelson Mandela, who has never been convicted of killing anyone, has now been in prison for more than ten years.

In the Cohen case, legal norms were reshaped throughout for the sake of clemency. The trial judge actually went beyond the evidence presented to arrive at a lenient judgment. At no stage was mitigating evidence adduced to suggest that Cohen killed his wife while mentally disturbed. In fact, the defense case was a complete denial that he had killed her. Maintaining this position throughout, his lawyers could hardly plead extenuating circumstances as a sort of fallback position, so it was entirely on the initiative of Judge A. Beyers that the extenuation was assumed. Judge Beyers had a guess at what had happened, and it was fortunate for Mr. Cohen that he did so, because this was a massive judicial unorthodoxy.

Then on top of this unusual method of arriving at a judgment came an unusual sentence. Twelve years is not a common sentence for murder in the absence of extenuating circumstance. In South Africa convicted murderers are usually hanged if there is no evidence in mitigation.

Murder is legally defined as the unlawful and intentional killing of a human being. Killing can be lawful, as in self-defense, war, or accident, when in the latter case the usual finding is culpable homicide if negligence is a factor. But in the Cohen case the finding was murder, implying the key element of intent to kill. That was why the twelve-year sentence was so unusual. Then Mr. Cohen went to prison and more surprises followed. The trial judge himself made representations for commutation of sentence, then the government granted reduction of the twelve-year sentence to five years.

That is all fine. I'm glad for Mr. Cohen and I'm all for leniency and in particular for the scrapping of the savage anachronism of capital punishment. But there should be more consistency in these matters. What about Nelson Mandela, for example? The government keeps denying that he is a political prisoner and maintains that he is a criminal. So let us treat him as another Ronald Cohen—a man convicted of a crime in a court of law.

Mandela was convicted of conspiring to overthrow the state by violent means, but there are three things to be said about this. Others once guilty of planning the same thing were soon freed by this same government, for example Robey Leibbrandt and other associates of Prime Minister Vorster in the outlawed OssewaBrandwag organization. Mandela has been in prison for more than ten years in the prime of his life. Finally, he is regarded by millions of black South Africans as their most important leader and could therefore play a key role in negotiating racial reconciliation in this country.

If this government can decide that a man convicted five years ago of murder must have done so under extreme provocation and should therefore be freed, can it not also decide the same about a man convicted ten years ago for planning actions he regarded as retaliation to extreme provocation?

Admittedly, instantaneous provocation is a more valid legal defense than general provocation, but provocation was at least pleaded by Mandela in his defense. It was never pleaded by Cohen.

There is every legal, moral, and political imperative for the freeing of Nelson Mandela, and also, for that matter, Robert Sobukwe, who is in his fifteenth year of state-imposed punishment and restriction for no crime more heinous than burning his passbook.

If the leaders of the present are more forgiving to the leaders of the future, perhaps one day the leaders of the future will be more forgiving to the leaders of the present.

# THE DAY
# THE FERTILIZER
# HIT THE FAN

*Hints in this article that government money was behind the bid of progovernment businessman Louis Luyt (pronounced "late") to buy an antiapartheid newspaper group were justified four years later when it was officially admitted that such funds had been provided by the Department of Information. The intention was to "tame" or close down the* Rand Daily Mail, *and this courageous newspaper was indeed closed down in 1985 by its proprietors, who claimed it was financially nonviable.*

So yet another attempt to take over South African Associated Newspapers has been blocked. A clear case of too little too Luyt. To some extent one can understand Mr. Louis Luyt's wish to get into the newspaper industry—it must be tough to go through life being described as a fertilizer king.

But there must be more to it than that. Why would an Afrikaner Nationalist businessman want to buy control of a chain of English-language newspapers persistently critical of the government Mr. Luyt so loyally supports? Or, to phrase it another way, why wouldn't he?

He must have had powerful friends supporting him for his bid even to become credible, because three previous attempts to take over the same company have been blocked at the level of the enigmatic man who controls the various groups owning Associated Newspapers—Mr. Clive Sinclair Corder of Cape Town.

An elderly gray-haired man who puffs profoundly at his pipe, Corder is the chief decision maker for the five major companies holding most of the company's shares, and he has the habit of hiding behind corporate aliases in conversation. Thus instead of saying: "I wouldn't be prepared to consider an offer for my company at this time," he says: "The Bailey Trusts and the other majority shareholders are unlikely to be receptive to an offer for Associated at this time."

One day I met him in Syfrets building, and as we had coffee I saw the Bailey Trusts lay down his pipe and light up a cigar for Majority Shareholders, which was then puffed on by Associated Proprietors. The smoke was exhaled by Union and Rhodesian Mining and the ash knocked off with a smile by Standard Bank Nominees.

It is not often you encounter such a plurality of personae in one man. And he is modest about it, which is remarkable if you consider that in terms of the doctrine of the Blessed Trinity even the Almighty is ascribed no more than three identities.

It has to be presumed, therefore, that Corder was the

final stumbling block in the path of Louis Luyt's bid to metamorphose from fertilizer king to press baron, and that liberal Johannesburg money was available to reinforce whatever reservations were jointly or severally held by Corder's various corporate identities.

And it was interesting to hear that the government favored Mr. Luyt's bid on the basis that his offer was a fair evaluation of the worth of the newspapers. So politics didn't come into it?

This tempts me to offer what I think is fair value for all the Afrikaans newspapers that support the government. I think I'll put in a bid for 450 rands for the lot, and in the style of Mr. Luyt I'll promise not to interfere with their editorial policies, provided they refrain from "writing things harmful to South Africa."

But the fuss and outrage unleashed when Mr. Luyt's takeover attempt blew up in his face was worth witnessing. What a day!

It may well go down as the day the fertilizer hit the fan.

# THE BALLAD OF
# FORT GLAMORGAN

*This article, written on December 26, 1975, related to
an attempt by General M. Geldenhuys to have me imprisoned on a technicality—refusal to disclose the
identity of a person sought by the security police.*

A funny thing happened to
me on my way to Christmas. Within twenty-four hours
I was (1) appointed to the Board of Sponsors of NICRO,
the National Institute for Crime Prevention and Reha-
bilitation of Offenders, and (2) sentenced to six months
imprisonment under Section 83 of the Criminal Proce-
dure Act.

The sentence, which is suspended pending appeal,
was imposed for refusal to reveal the identity of a person who stated that he had witnessed criminal actions
by the security police. Because the appeal is pending,

nothing may be published about the merits of the case, but several general observations can be made.

One is that if the appeal fails I'll be in a position to observe prison conditions from both sides of the bars, so to speak. In my capacity as a NICRO official I'll inspect prison facilities from the outside looking in, then in my capacity as a prisoner I'll compare these impressions with the view from the inside looking out. There's in-depth reporting for you.

Later I'll co-opt other ex-prisoners, such as Prime Minister Balthazar Vorster and the head of the Bureau of State Security, General Hendrik Van den Bergh, so that we veterans of the cells can advise NICRO on the basis of practical experience.

The prison to which I am provisionally consigned is the region's main penitentiary, Fort Glamorgan. It is a forbidding-looking redoubt high above the wooded banks of the Buffalo River. Last Christmas I donated a chess set to Fort Glamorgan for the prisoners, little suspecting I might one day have cause to be grateful for my own generosity.

I've already inspected the accommodation and it leaves a lot to be desired. And that, of course, is the section for whites. The section for blacks is even more medieval. Fortunately the outfit with stripes or little arrows is now out of fashion. The garb now is a sort of off-white tunic.

I had coffee with the head warder, after making an appointment to check out the facilities, and he was apologetic about the condition of the cells and the plumbing. Fort Glamorgan is one of the oldest prisons in South Africa, not a slick five-star set-up like Pretoria Central.

But there are possibilities. Oscar Wilde wrote some of his best stuff in Reading Gaol, and maybe I'll be able to turn out something along the lines of "The Ballad of Fort Glamorgan" in between the library duties to which I understand I might be assigned.

Anyway, there are several months to go yet before my appeal can be heard, so the authorities at Fort Glamorgan mustn't be surprised if a more than usually zealous NICRO official keeps calling to check on the standard of food the prisoners are getting.

And I'm prepared to be generous about the whole thing. If the leading lights of our government ensure that I'm not too badly treated if I have to go inside, I promise to put in a good word for them one day when the tribunals begin in South Africa.

# WHERE TIME
# STANDS STILL

*Most South Africans never see snow, but there are some remote mountainous areas of the country that sometimes have snow and become "ski resorts" for the intrepid few who are prepared to travel there. Such a place is where mining magnate Cecil Rhodes once had a farm, and the village still bears his name.*

The tiny village of Rhodes in the northeast corner of the Cape Province up in the mountains by the Lesotho border reminds one of Brigadoon. Time seems to have stood still there.

It's a long drive from anywhere, but the effort is worth it. The scenery improves the closer you get, until it becomes quite spectacular. Clear trout streams run through craggy mountains and bright green valleys fringed with giant poplars and cypresses.

The village at first looks like a film set—too good to be true. It is crammed with quaint little houses in architectural styles of the last century, with ogee roofs over the verandahs, and the occasional porch roofed in the bullnose fashion, curving downward to the drainage gutter.

The houses are in a variety of colors and are referred to by color—the yellow house, the blue house, the red house—because there are so few of them. In fact, Rhodes has more houses than people. There are only thirty-seven inhabitants, but about fifty houses. The unoccupied ones belong to people from as far afield as Johannesburg and Cape Town who stumbled on the place, fell in love with it, and wanted to own a piece of it for occasional holidays there.

The main attractions are trout fishing in summer and skiing in winter and a mysterious charm about the village itself. Apart from the quaint houses, Rhodes is distinctive for its massive and numerous trees, including an enormous weeping willow bigger than any I've seen. There is also the poignancy of a once-brisk little community reduced by the migration of young people to the cities, illustrated by the school building that once had 100 pupils and now has none, and an old stone church seldom used, with a churchyard like an illustration for Gray's "Elegy."

The leading citizen of Rhodes is Meneer Buytendag, an old gentleman with a variety of civic capacities. He is acting mayor, acting tourist officer, acting estate agent, and chief trout spotter, with all the information you need to know about the village, past and present. It is unthinkable to call him Mister Buytendag or to speak English to him—you'd be missing an authentic experience of the old Afrikaner courtliness that echoes a more gracious age.

Many years ago a certain Van den Horst came to Rhodes and boarded with a bearded patriarch and his family. There being nothing to do in the evenings, the old man and his five sons would sit around the perimeter of the sitkamer after supper, smoking and saying nothing. Well, almost nothing, because every now and then the old man would take his pipe out of his mouth, sigh deeply, and say: "Ja, nee." Whereupon one of his sons would respectfully respond: "Ja, Pa!"

Somehow the Afrikaans phrase "Yes, no" is far more eloquent than its tame English equivalent "Ho-hum."

So don't go to Rhodes in search of glittering conversation or bright lights. But be prepared for the occasional surprise. The rustic traditions are strong, and one Christmas a friend was shocked out of his sleep by what sounded like a shouting horde of invaders from Lesotho. But it was only a party of local mummers singing carols from house to house. Suddenly it could have been an old-time village in Wessex, with the tranter and the chandler in the choir. But in spite of his rude awakening, my friend says Rhodes is usually a place of such utter silence that he can hear the stars.

Without quite hearing the music of the spheres in this enchanted village, I recently spent a week there and didn't have a moment of boredom.

Who could be bored in Brigadoon?

# KONKORDAT WITH THE KREMLIN

*The bogey of communism was used so often by the South African government that it was no surprise when a member of the cabinet suggested I was furthering the aims of the Soviet Union. This prompted the following article by way of reply.*

Our government spends so much time saving us from the Soviets that one wonders why, in view of the extent of common ground between Pretoria and the Kremlin.

Both governments put state authority above civil rights.
Both believe in imprisonment without trial.
Both withhold the vote from the majority.
Both punish dissidents with banning and banishment.
Both reject the liberal concept of individual liberty.

48

Both exercise political censorship over the arts.
Both restrict the news coverage of the media.
Both impose systems of ideological education.
Both use house arrest as a state punishment.
Both prohibit the free movement of citizens.
Both punish critics by withdrawing their passports.
Both rely heavily on the marketing of gold and dia-
monds.

Yes, the two regimes share many values.

There are, however, some differences in approach. In
the Soviet Union all television, radio, and newspapers
are under state control, whereas here in South Africa
state control is limited to all radio, television, and about
half the newspapers. Also, here in South Africa, the
level of state monopoly is not quite as high as in the
Soviet Union. Our state monopolies such as Iscor (steel),
Sasol (oil), Escom (electricity), railways, airways, and
many para-statal entities such as the XDC, are not yet
as all-pervasive as in Russia.

From what one reads there is more freedom in Russia
for the average citizen compared with that of the black
South African here, and somewhat less for the average
Russian compared with the average white South African. One gathers that the restrictions in Russia as to
who may play sport with whom, who may live next to
whom, who may marry or sleep with whom, and who
may share a park bench with whom are less onerous
than in South Africa. And no doubt many examples of
the opposite could be found.

The final similarity between the South African government and the Kremlin is that fewer than 10 percent of Russians are members of the ruling party there and fewer than 10 percent of South Africans are members of the ruling party here—yet another reason why both regimes spend a lot of money on internal security.

In view of all this common ground, why doesn't our government seek an alliance with Moscow? In these days of increasing isolation the sole friendship of dictator Stroessner of Paraguay is little comfort.

The snag is that the Kremlin would probably reject such an overture. Their image is bad enough already, and they wouldn't want to make it worse.

# HE SANK
# A WARSHIP

*This article was carefully structured to hold the main point right back to the end. It provoked controversy and highlighted the fact that the war hero it was about had been buried not in Heroes' Acre, Pretoria, but in a pauper's grave.*

In these military days when complacent politicians utter heroic speeches while the young have to face the real bullets, it is worth recalling what real heroes are like. One of our greatest South African war heroes was a young man who destroyed, single-handedly, a German warship in Tobruk harbor during World War II.

He was a prisoner of war, having served with the Second South African Division in Egypt when he was captured by the Germans. Sitting in a barbed-wire compound at Tobruk, absently digging his fingers into the warm sand behind him, he touched something: a cartridge. This gave him an idea, and he dug around until he had several dozen. He emptied the cordite from them into a powdered-milk can, and further search in the sand revealed some lengths of fuse, which he joined together and concealed with the cordite. He was going to make a bomb and blow up an enemy ship.

Day after day he and other prisoners of war were marched to the harbor to unload the ships, and his chance to use the bomb came when he and several others were taken by barge to a ship anchored out in the bay.

Their task was to load ammunition and drums of fuel, and he asked his companions to distract the German guards shortly before they were to return to the compound at sundown. While they did so by staging a scuffle, he climbed down into the hold, took out his little "bomb" and placed it among several drums of fuel, laying the fuse to within a few feet of the hatch above his head.

He opened a can of gasoline and poured it over the "bomb" and the surrounding fuel drums, then scrambled back on deck where his friends were being cuffed with rifle-butts for "accidentally" dropping a box of ammunition into the water. He stayed near the hatch until the guards ordered the prisoners back to the barge, then bent as if to tie a shoelace, struck a match, and touched off the fuse.

The guards and prisoners were all clear of the ship when she blew up in a huge explosion, and although all the prisoners were interrogated, the Germans decided it wasn't sabotage. Several nights later the young saboteur crept through the wire and escaped from Tobruk, rejoining the South African forces near El Alamein after walking for twenty-three days.

He was later awarded the Military Medal for his feat.

His name was Job Masego.

The companions who helped him by diverting the guards were Andrew Mohudi, Samuel Masiya, Jacob Shawe, Sam Polisi, and Ralph Ridgard.

Yes, you can tell by the names that they were of the category of South African soldiers who were not allowed to carry weapons, but were there to serve the white troops.

# WON'T YOU COME HOME, PIET BEUKES?

*Most Afrikaans-language newspapers had for so long been owned and controlled by the governing Afrikaner Nationalist Party that there was a dull conformity in their journalism—with, however, one notable exception. . . .*

In this crisis year of 1976 when news headlines reflect more cause for depression than amusement, we need the irreverent touch of Piet Beukes in our journalism. Maybe not his whole approach to the job, but just that touch. . . .

Piet Beukes, many will recall, was the maverick among Afrikaner journalists who broke out of the whole somber partylining mold of the Afrikaans-language press and founded the rip-roaring, disreputable mass-circulation weekly, *Landstem*, based on sin, sex, and sensation. And the Volk lapped it up, whereas the Volk Establishment hurried to buy him out before he could turn the masses rebellious.

Today the graying Beukes, looking like an elderly version of movie director Mel Brooks, chuckles when quizzed about his more bizarre escapades. One of his front-page lead stories related the demise of an elderly farmer who lit his pipe in his outdoor toilet, which contained a build-up of methane gas. The resulting explosion was splashed across nine columns in *Landstem* in morbid detail.

Beukes didn't believe in routine introductions carrying the basic facts first, such as: "A seventy-eight-year-old farmer, Isak van Rensburg, was killed when methane gas exploded in his outdoor toilet on the farm Ontploffingsfontein, near Kroonstad yesterday." No, Beukes liked to build up the drama first, in a folksy way, so his story would begin: "Look, Oom Sakkie always enjoyed a pipe on his visits to his privy . . ."

The reader was then led by the hand along the fateful path followed that morning by the unsuspecting Oom Sakkie on his appointment with destiny in the doomed loo. The tamping down of the tobacco, the contented settling on the seat, the ruminative production of a match, these would all be related in loving detail. Then, like a conductor leading his orchestra into a tutti crescendo, Beukes would unleash on the reader the full force of the regrettable explosion that followed. And, in a Beukes master touch, this imaginative account would be flanked by a straightfaced scientific account from the *Landstem*'s science editor on the explosive properties of methane gas when exposed to naked flame.

Ah, yes, something colorful if not exquisitely tasteful went out of South African journalism when Piet Beukes hung up his scurrilous pen. Once he published what purported to be an exclusive interview with Russia's leading space scientist, Professor Blagonravov, which contained hair-raising claims of what the Soviets would do to the Americans in space. The news agencies picked up the story, which flew around the world and touched off a superpower row. Beukes was bombarded with phone calls and cables from all over the world, including the U.S. State Department and finally the angry Blagonravov himself, who knew nothing of any interview with anyone and had never heard of Beukes or *Landstem*.

Challenged about this by friends, Beukes said indignantly: "It's what the bugger *would* have said if he'd been interviewed!" And the front page banner lead in the next issue of *Landstem* was: RUSSIANS ATTACK LANDSTEM!

Like a sort of Afrikaner Dickens, Beukes peopled his pages with characters and events larger than life, and if their words and deeds owed less to fact than to the vivid Beukes imagination, they caused less harm than the usual untruths in the government-owned Afrikaans newspapers.

Maybe he'll make a comeback. His readers would surely love to be able to thrill once again to phrases like: "In an exclusive telephone call to the White House last night . . ." (omitting to explain that it was simply to the White House operator) or "I understand from private sources at Buckingham Palace that . . ."

There's another reason why his descriptive powers are needed at this time. The apartheid policy is leading this country relentlessly, and, considering the nature of that policy, appropriately, toward the fate suffered by Oom Sakkie in his rustic outhouse.

Someone will have to record the explosion.

Piet Beukes! Where are you now that your country really needs you?

# TOO LATE FOR QUESTIONS

*The South Africa Foundation was formed by business-men to promote a "positive" image of South Africa abroad and to attract overseas investment, but as the years passed its senior members realized that a positive image abroad was incompatible with apartheid at home. To try to nudge the government toward reform they started listing questions being asked abroad, such as: "Why don't blacks have the vote?;" "Why do blacks have to carry passes?;" and "Why are blacks not allowed to travel freely around South Africa?"*

D̲r. Jan Marais, president of the South Africa Foundation, has been asking some more questions. Two years ago he listed fifty questions asked by international critics of apartheid, and last week he posed seventeen questions he said South Africans should ask themselves about the future.

Dr. Marais is one of several prominent Afrikaner Nationalists who pass on such questions as the diplomatic way of criticizing state policy without seeming to be disloyal. Their motives are admirable, but they ask too many questions. They should stop asking questions and start giving answers.

There is one simple answer to all the questions about this country's major problems—apartheid. This is what Dr. Marais and his fellow questioners should be using their establishment influence to say. They should be telling their friends in power to scrap apartheid, and that the only way to scrap apartheid is to scrap apartheid.

There isn't time for all this tiptoe tact. When a wall is collapsing on you there isn't scope for subtlety—you have to move fast.

But the questioners are locked into the political incestuousness of governing party politics. They still imagine that the major power struggle going on in South Africa is between the left wing and the right wing of the governing party.

But the major power struggle in South Africa today is not even between white Afrikaner Nationalists and the white opposition, nor even between whites and blacks as such. The ultimate issue is between blacks and blacks—between conservative blacks and radical blacks. And the radical blacks are winning.

The conservatives, like Chief Gatsha Buthelezi and other "homeland" leaders, are trying to hold the black center with as conciliatory a policy for whites as they feel is consonant with black aspirations, and for this they are increasingly being seen by the black majority as collaborationist.

Who leads the radical blacks? The answer is legion. Many of the leaders are banned, restricted, imprisoned, or underground, but many are not, and they function in all the major townships and the rural areas as well. Hard-line black consciousness is now their stock-in-trade, and they are closely in touch with black Africa.

Whites, seeing only the tip of the iceberg that is the ultimate black power struggle, believe that the only black leaders with large followings are the ones whose names appear often in the headlines. Accordingly they see Buthelezi not as an ally but as if he represents the main body of black opposition to apartheid.

That body is hydra-headed, and the more heads chopped off by banning, the more they proliferate. So throughout the country, right under the unsuspecting noses of whites, the future rulers of South Africa are flexing their political muscles.

Meanwhile, what are whites debating? Whether cricketers of varying skin pigmentation can play on the same field, or whether some of Dr. Marais's sixty-seven questions might offend the right-wingers in the cabinet!

That it's too late for questions there is no doubt.

Let us hope it's not too late for answers.

# BOOBS BETTER THAN BOO-BOOS

*This article, published in April 1976, followed a spate of government speeches linking permissiveness, rock music, long hair, and short skirts with Communist designs to corrupt South African youth and promote interracial sex. One government official, in particular, regarded a topless scene in a play as just what the Kremlin ordered.*

The Administrator of Cape Province, Dr. Lapa Munnik, is horrified at the baring of bosoms on stage and regards such permissiveness as part of a Communist conspiracy to undermine the morals of the nation.

Whether or not bare boobs boost Bolshevism, it would be better for the nation if people like Dr. Munnik worried more about administrative boo-boos.

For example, Dr. Munnik as the man responsible for the provincial hospital services should have addressed himself to the following problems:

The budget for construction of Tygerberg Hospital was 12 million rands. So far it has cost 60 million, and they're not finished yet.

The corridors were designed wide enough to allow two patient gurneys to pass each other, but someone forgot to make the doors wide enough to admit even one gurney.

The expensive decor in the wards included polyvinyl wall covering, but after this was installed someone realized that in conditions of heat this gives off poisonous fumes. Down came the expensive covering.

Then there were the fancy door handles, designed so that a nurse carrying a tray could open any door with her elbow. The only snag was that they were all installed upside down, so if you see a lot of Tygerberg nurses learning that upward karate kick, it is to enable them to open doors.

In the five-story operating block all the windows were installed upside down, then taken out and put in correctly. Then someone realized the place was designed for fixed windows because of the air-conditioning system, so out they came again for fixed windows to be installed.

Doctors working at Tygerberg say that one storeroom door was relocated eleven times, and there are other stories of boo-boos that haven't been possible to verify.

With this sort of administrative planning, who needs Communist conspiracies to undermine a country?

Another major hospital in Cape Province is Frere Hospital in East London, recently expanded at enormous cost. Yet the expanded hospital now handles fewer operations than the old one did and can't function at the previous level of efficiency because there aren't enough nurses.

Is this because of a shortage of nurses in the area? Not at all. There are many highly trained unemployed nurses available—but they're the wrong shade of skin color. In other words, people will be segregated even if it kills them. Presumably there are thousands of white patients dying to be exclusive.

And, also in the interests of racial segregation, there is a new multimillion-rand hospital for blacks in the nearby township of Mdantsane, but it can't open for business because it has no doctors.

So as we, the taxpayers, reflect on this 1,400-bed hospital now being run as a 42-bed clinic, we might decide that it, like the boo-boo at Frere Hospital and the multiple boo-boos at Tygerberg, are considerably more distressing to us than Dr. Munnik's eccentric theories about the ideological aspects of mammary revelation.

# SEE THE HOWLER
# MONKEY

*By May 1976 there had been so many verbal attacks*
*by government speakers on Helen Suzman and her few*
*antiapartheid colleagues of the Progressive Party that*
*the campaign was clearly orchestrated.*

The South American howl-
er monkey uses its highly developed vocal soundbox
as a defense mechanism when threatened. The more
frightened it becomes, the louder it howls, assailing the
eardrum to the point of physical pain.

Today in South Africa the howler monkey has a political counterpart—the apartheid politician who sees at
last that his government is under threat.

Unlike the howler monkey, however, he doesn't recognize the real threat—in his case from militant
blacks—but stays locked into past political patterns,

64

which portray the main threat as coming from moderate whites.

For many years the lone voice of Helen Suzman in the South African parliament seemed a luxury he could afford, unwelcome though it was, because there was only one of her. But when she began to be joined by other Progressives our howler monkey began to get nervous. Suddenly white renegades were no longer so freakish.

And as there came to be more Progressives, there came to be more howler monkeys, and their howls started to grow in volume. Their tree was being invaded by strange beings, the more dangerous because they looked like them. Today the voice of the political howler monkey is the standard noise proceeding from our parliament.

One howl is to the effect that the tree "cannot afford" such creatures. Another avers that they hate the tree itself. Yet another is to the effect that the interlopers will be "the first to get their throats cut" when the tree is uprooted.

Suddenly there is a new crisis of perception! If the tree is uprootable, the existence of potential uprooters has to be acknowledged!

Now come the loudest howls of all . . .

But the thing to remember, as the howler monkey syndrome develops, is that the vocal mechanism employed by the creature in this way is essentially defensive. The howl is loudest when the howler is in retreat.

And whereas in its final frenzy the howler monkey

can do considerable damage to the eardrum, its preoc-cupation with fear makes it essentially a negative crea-ture.

The present pattern of encroachment into its tree en-sures that in terms of its own concept of the political jungle it faces a future of ever-diminishing returns.

# DACHAU
# EXPLAINED TO
# CHILDREN

*Toward the middle of 1976 there was national argu-*
*ment over the screening of the series "The World at*
*War" on South African television. Many government*
*supporters claimed that scenes showing Nazi concen-*
*tration camps would upset children, but the real rea-*
*son for their objection was their lingering sympathy*
*for the Nazi cause. The British makers of the series*
*stood firm against such cuts and the scenes were*
*shown.*

**M**any South Africans be-
lieved the "World at War" episode dealing with Hitler's
death camps shouldn't have appeared on our television
screens. They claimed this was because they didn't
want their children to see it. . . .

Taking the opposite view, I watched it with my children, and for those who don't know how to explain such
atrocities I offer the following approach:

You can't understand why the Nazis murdered all
those people? Well, it all starts with prejudice. Prejudice means judging people without knowing them; hav-

ing hostile feelings toward people without sensible reason; regarding people as part of a group instead of as individuals.

Prejudice is like a disease, and children usually catch it from parents and other adults. But it can be prevented through good education, and sometimes it can be cured with psychiatric treatment.

Hitler didn't have a good education, and he grew up prejudiced against Jews. He was never cured of this prejudice because he never had proper treatment. He found that many other people had the same prejudice against Jews, so he became leader of Germany by spreading scare stories about Jews and by promising to save Germany from them. Eventually he told his followers to kill all the Jews, and that's why there were places like Dachau.

Why didn't they refuse? Well, in a nondemocracy people don't ask questions when they are told what to do. They just do it. If they don't they are called disloyal to the country. Yes, a dictatorship is the opposite of a democracy. A dictator is a person who is scared of most of his own countrymen and that is why he won't let them vote.

Why didn't someone report Hitler to the police? In a dictatorship you don't have proper police. You have political police. Proper police fight crime. Political police fight political opponents of the government. Yes, Hitler used to imprison people without trial. He used to ban and banish them and house-arrest them. He regarded people who disagreed with him as enemies of the whole country.

No, he didn't really believe they were, or he would have let judges decide, wouldn't he? Dictators play on the fears of ignorant people. Hitler knew how much his people feared communism, so he called people who disagreed with him Communists. In that way he got many of his followers to believe that good people were bad people, that bad things were good things and that lies were truth.

Yes, there were many people here who admired Hitler in those days. Some are in our government today. But they weren't the government of South Africa then. Our government in those days declared war against Hitler. Yes, the present government came to power in 1948.

What is a patriot? A patriot is someone who wants the best for his country, including the best laws and the best ideals. It's something other people should call you—you shouldn't call yourself that. People who call themselves patriots are usually liars. A wise man, Dr. Johnson, once said that patriotism is the last refuge of a scoundrel. He meant that people who praise their own love of country are usually covering up their lack of it.

Yes, it is unpatriotic to love the things in your country that are wrong. When Dachau death camp was built, Hitler's men put up a sign outside it: MY COUNTRY, RIGHT OR WRONG.

Those are among the most evil words ever written.

# DAMPIE, DAMPIE, SLUK, SLUK

*This was a commentary on one of the few nonconform-*
*ist articles in the Afrikaans-language press, a dig at*
*the propensity of government-controlled media to cen-*
*sor out news unfavorable or unwelcome to white*
*South Africans. Boxing fans had to rely on radio com-*
*mentaries because television as a matter of policy*
*didn't cover professional boxing live. The word Uit-*
*landers means foreigners.*

I must share with English-
speaking readers one of the funniest articles yet to appear in the Afrikaans press. Written by Andries Van
Wyk of *Rapport*, it describes the victory of the Argen-
tinian boxer, Victor Galindez, over our own Pierre
Fourie in a world title bout.

Van Wyk describes how he established himself next
to his radio with brandy and cigarettes near to hand,
and how he switched back and forth from the English-
language commentary to the Afrikaans-language one for
the sake of stereolingual balance, as it were.

He punctuates his account with the words "dampie" (puff) and "sluk" (sip), as he has increasing recourse to the brandy and cigarettes during the divergent commentaries.

During the initial rounds he stays with Morkel Van Tonder and Gerhard Viviers as these two commentators describe Fourie pounding Galindez all around the ring. Dampie. Sluk.

Then he switches over to the English transmission, where he is disquieted to hear Bert Blewett and Trevor Quirk telling a somewhat different story. They have Galindez constantly on the attack against a defensive Fourie, who is landing only occasional punches. Dampie, dampie.

Back to the Afrikaans transmission, and all is again well, with Fourie well ahead on points. Sluk. Then in spite of actually hearing over the radio the impact of a dreadful body blow from Galindez, he receives the information that Fourie has danced out of the way of it. This worries him enough to send him back to the English transmission, where our Pierre is being clobbered all over the ring. Sluk, dampie, sluk, dampie.

In the fourteenth round, says the puzzled Van Wyk, there is an even greater discrepancy between the two accounts, sluk, sluk, sluk. Blewett and Quirk have Galindez swarming all over Fourie, whereas Viviers and Van Tonder have Fourie skillfully weathering a desperate attack.

Morkel Van Tonder predicts a points victory for Fourie. Viviers agrees that Fourie is so far ahead that only a knockout in the last round can rob him of a unanimous decision.

Over to the English transmission, where Fourie is already almost out on his feet and the commentators are speculating on whether he can last the distance. Dampie, dampie, sluk, sluk.

By now desperately worried, Van Wyk foreswears the English transmission entirely and stays with his fellow Afrikaners for the last round.

To his delight he hears that Fourie has won; that Fourie is the world champion! Well, that is the verdict of Morkel Van Tonder and Gerhard Viviers (by now being referred to as "Gerhard" and "Morkel") who prepare to interview Fourie on his victory as the judges hand in their decisions to the referee.

Then comes the bombshell—Galindez has won!

Over on the English-language transmission there is no surprise at this decision, but back on the Afrikaans-language one there is chaos and uproar, until finally Van Tonder points out that two of the three judges are from overseas.

Well, there you are, concludes Van Wyk with a plethora of dampies and sluks as he reflects on these foreign referees:

"The Uitlanders have committed yet another injustice on the Boers!"

# A CASE
# FOR SHERLOCK

*A night watchman hired by my newspaper to guard my house saw security police officers G. Cilliers and J. Van Wyk drive away after firing shots at the front of my house. In South Africa the security police (political) are often called Special Branch. In spite of evidence tendered in this case, the uniformed police declined to investigate the issue.*

One morning this week at 4:30 A.M. five bullets were fired at the front of my house. First one shot was fired, then four in rapid succession, from an accelerating car. Beside the intrepid gunman, who was at the wheel, sat a man clutching an empty spray-paint canister. He had used it to write several slogans on the wall.

Shortly before midnight they had phoned my wife to say they knew she was alone because I was out of town and that they would be coming to "get" her. Actually she wasn't alone. Our five children, ranging in age from thirteen to four, were also in the house. But one knows what "they" meant.

Approached for a comment on this attack, the Minister of Police, James T. Kruger, said he presumed the police were investigating and declined to comment further. And since Mr. Kruger presumes the police are investigating, let us presume to help the police with some Sherlock Holmes deduction.

My dear Watson, it shouldn't be too difficult to discover the culprits. The field is narrowed down considerably by the fact that those who telephoned their threat said enough to indicate they had overheard several of her phone conversations that evening, and here in South Africa telephone-tapping equipment is restricted to very few.

What, Watson? You say anyone could have overheard such conversations if the lines were crossed? Ah, you must always look for the extra dimension, my dear fellow. Here the extra dimension is the word *Biko*, because shortly before leaving on my trip I had a conversation with Steve Biko, and if you look at the words painted on my wall you will read first BIKO, then the strangely spelled COMMY HQ.

This indicates an obsession with communism, because only obsessed persons imply that non-Communists are Communists. Do we know any agency that equates criticism of the government with communism? Is such "communism" viewed as a threat to their security, Watson? Aha!

Now consider the misspelling of the word *commy—*

would an English-speaking person be likely to spell it that way? So we look for a person with the equipment to listen in on calls to an unlisted number, who does not spell well in English, who is obsessed with communism, and who resents my friendship with Steve Biko. Do we happen to know such a man, Watson? Elementary, old chap!

And does he have a close associate in the same line of work? Anything Special about their work? What sort of people are issued with .635-caliber pistols? Remember that all such pistols are licensed in this country, so some interesting investigation into license records could be done, couldn't it, Watson?

We have Police Minister Kruger's presumption that the police are investigating, and as we know, Watson, the police are uniquely well-qualified to trace this attack.

Yes, I know that there are many such attacks on critics of government policy and it is odd that no culprits have been arrested and charged for such crimes.

Yes, I know it seems wrong that no member of the government has condemned such acts of terrorism.

But be fair, Watson. Police Minister Kruger and his colleagues are very busy people and they have to give priority to more important things.

Like stopping Sunday movies in Natal.

# THE SIGNALS FROM SOWETO

*The Soweto uprising began as a peaceful protest march by black schoolchildren who objected to being taught in the Afrikaans language, which they regarded as the language of apartheid oppression. But when police opened fire on them, the schoolchildren fought back with sticks, stones, and bottles, in pitched battles that went on for more than ten days. Hundreds were killed, but Soweto was never "tame" again.*

To say the Soweto riots were over Afrikaans-language instruction in black schools is like saying the American war of independence was over the stamp tax. Each was merely the trigger issue in a boiling-up of wider resentments and in each case official arrogance was to blame.

Police Minister James T. Kruger said he had been expecting something of the sort to happen. Well, hadn't we all? Mr. Kruger also spoke of the dangers of black consciousness giving way to black power. But who started all this color consciousness? Wasn't it the people who started segregating park benches in this country? Wasn't it the people who brought in laws emphasizing race?

Mr. Kruger speaks of agitators in Soweto. But don't agitators agitate most agitatedly when there is deep discontent? And how does all this square with the government's oft-repeated claim that race relations have never been better? And how does it square with official anger against those of us who warn that race relations have never been worse?

Mr. Kruger says blacks should accept the good faith and sincerity of whites, but when are we going to see concrete evidence of such good faith? As to sincerity, no one was being more sincere than Salty du Rand when he punched Morne du Plessis during the rugby final at Ellis Park last Saturday.

Sincerity alone is not enough. What matters is what one is being sincere about.

Good faith can also have its shortcomings. If you play tennis against someone who isn't allowed to use a backhand or forehand and may not serve or volley, it doesn't mean anything to say you play such a match in good faith.

In this country the black majority aren't allowed to vote, to campaign against unjust laws, to support mass movements of popular choice, to object lawfully and effectively to such harsh measures, or to take part in normal political activity.

Soweto is one of the results, and there will be many others.

Meanwhile Mr. Kruger and his cabinet colleagues should really stop using that phrase about their patience being exhausted. The last chap who was partial to it ended up in a bombed bunker in Berlin.

Besides, patience is a two-way commodity in South Africa, and judging by the way violent protest spread from Soweto, there are millions of blacks whose patience is also exhausted.

# ALL COMMISSIONS
# ACCEPTED HERE

*The South African government often set up govern-*
*mental commissions of inquiry in order to close off*
*public inquiry—once governmental commissions were*
*announced on any issue that issue was declared sub*
*judice, precluding comment or discussion until the*
*commission declared its findings.*

It took the Theron Commission three years and a lot of money and effort to report what anyone could have told the government in less than a minute—that the "colored" people want apartheid abolished and their vote restored.

What are all these commissions of inquiry really for?

Take the commission of inquiry Prime Minister Vorster appointed when a newspaper reported that his son-in-law had received a large loan from the Land Bank. I could have checked that for Mr. Vorster in the Land

Bank records within a day. Then take the Press Commission, which sat for eleven years before deciding that the South African newspapers are law-abiding and non-subversive. Hell, I could have told the government that right away.

Then take the Schlebush Commission. Surely everyone knew no student leaders had broken any law and that the only way to stop them campaigning against apartheid would be to ban them. The Snyman and De Vriess Commissions could also have been dispensed with in five minutes.

Look, I've got nothing against commissions of inquiry as such. Some of my best friends are commissions of inquiry.

But the way this government uses commissions of inquiry is absurd. When it suits them to take the heat off an issue they appoint a commission, then decline all questions on the grounds that this would be preempting the findings of the inquiry, then protract the inquiry proceedings as long as possible.

If the commission reports what the government wants it to report, which it generally does because it is government appointed, the government accepts the "findings." But if something goes wrong and the commission reports in a manner that doesn't suit the government, the commission's findings are rejected. What could be more convenient?

If ever the government wants some real commission proceedings, I'll be glad to help out. There are many issues a one-man commission could settle overnight in this country.

So, just to be helpful, this is to announce that from now on all commissions will be readily undertaken, at far less cost to the taxpayer.

In fact, for you as a friend, wholesale!

# PUSSYFOOTS
# IN THE PULPIT

*Most white clergymen in South Africa were so con-*
*servative on racial matters that the question of*
*apartheid never cropped up in their sermons. Congre-*
*gations reflected the segregation laws—there were*
*black congregations in black townships and white*
*congregations in white suburbs.*

Every week hundreds of thousands of white South Africans attend Christian churches, but the sermons they hear have little to do with Christianity in this country. Most of the clergymen are too scared of real Christianity to spell out its requirements.

For nearly two thousand years Christianity has posed a special challenge to one country after another. In Rome it was up against Nero; in Germany it was up against nazism; in Italy it was up against fascism. In South Africa it should be up against apartheid.

But among whites, with very few exceptions, our pulpits are crammed with pussyfoots. They will preach against anything but apartheid. There it is, but they look the other way. They step carefully around the huge moral boulder to point to tiny pebbles of theology in other directions. They will thunder out boldly against any number of lesser evils, giving chapter, verse, book, and parable. Meticulously they will identify the mote in the parish eye—but the beam in the nation's eye is treated as being above criticism.

If they are simply nervous, fair enough. There's a lot to be nervous about. But then they should get out of their pulpits and find other jobs. As Harry Truman said: "If you can't stand the heat, stay out of the kitchen."

When you listen to the constant stream of bland baloney that is intoned over the radio in the name of religion, it is obvious that the state broadcasting authorities are vetting the stuff before it goes out, and that the clerics are collaborating with the requirement that in South Africa Christianity has to be noncontroversial.

Not that the radio preachers are disseminating unsound theology. Oh no. It is sound theology all right—just massively irrelevant. If someone's house is burning down and your response is to advise him to drive carefully on major highways, this is sound advice. It just doesn't happen to be relevant to his major problem.

And that's what our pulpit pussyfoots do about apartheid. They talk about everything else—sex, alcohol, drugs, theft, and all manner of naughtinesses but the main one, the big one, the one that stares us in the face every day in South Africa.

You've got to hand it to these dauntless Expounders of the Word—the sheer skill with which they avoid the major moral issue of our time and place is remarkable. And if they should touch tangentially upon it it is in such vague and general terms that their congregations can read their own interpretations into what is said and unsaid.

For example, they will say that Christians should pay their workers a fair wage, and the faithful, paying a lousy 30 rands a month, will nod complacently because they have decided this is a fair wage. What should be said from the pulpit is that according to the research of Stellenbosch University, which is hardly a radical institution, the poverty datum line in South Africa today is 85 rands a month, and any wage below that is theft.

Another thing that should be said is that no person who votes for or supports any political party that deprives human beings of their rights on the basis of skin pigmentation has any business in a Christian church.

When ministers of religion fail to spell out such basic morality, their congregations are entitled to demand equal vagueness about murder, adultery, fraud, and debauchery. And if the Ten Commandments can be overruled by parliamentary statute or individual interpretation, at least all the churchgoers will know where they stand.

But here in South Africa at this time it is obscene to hear a preacher intoning from a pulpit that all must take up the cross, while failing to mention that more than 20 million South Africans are already doing this without choice, by statutory compulsion, because they were born with dark skins.

Every pulpit in South Africa should have a basin of water and a towel, so that every time a pussyfooting preacher chickens out he can wash his hands in tribute to his real hero—Pontius Pilate.

# HIGH PRIESTS
# OF OUTRAGE

*The reaction to the previous article was heatedly de-*
*fensive. Many church ministers and preachers tried to*
*justify themselves by saying they they had to be "non-*
*political."*

Last week's article on
"Pussyfoots in the Pulpit" drew outraged objections
from clergymen and their fellow travelers all over the
country. They say that apartheid is politics, and preachers should steer clear of politics.

Now isn't that dandy? So if politicians passed a law
making public adultery compulsory among consenting
adults, presumably our clergymen would refrain from
comment on what would now be a political issue. . . .

You know what these High Priests of Outrage are saying, of course—that politics is somehow more sacred

than morality. And when they talk of steering clear of "politics" they obviously mean "opposition" politics. To commend the government in a radio sermon is somehow nonpolitical, while to condemn it would be political.

When the genuine churchmen, like Beyers Naude or Archbishop Denis Hurley, do what the rest should be doing, the Scribes and Pharisees are the first to mutter about "controversy" and there being a "right way and a wrong way of putting something." Can't you just hear how that other High Priest, Caiaphas, might have put it: "Come, come, Christ, it's not so much what you are saying but the way you are saying it. Prudence, my dear chap—there's a way of doing these things."

Yes, and there's a way of *not* doing these things. Here is where the pulpit pussyfoots have become expert in evolving their own version of the Ten Commandments: "Thou shalt not steal, unless it be through property expropriations under the Group Areas Act; Thou shalt not bear false witness, unless thou belongest to the security police; Thou shalt not kill, unless thou interrogatest dissidents in detention . . ."

And because their role is essentially phoney, they have adopted a whole range of phoney intonations and artificial pronunciations. They play vocal games, letting the voice drop toward the end of the sentence, pronouncing "comfort" as though it rhymed with "some fought" and "evil" as "eeveel" and "Christ" as "Chroyst."

The Afrikaans-speaking ones playing similar games

affect an elimination of the normal double *e* sound so that "gees" rhymes not with "pierce" but with "peace," and several have cultivated an incantatory style of delivery in which the voice breaks emotionally on the high notes.

Their style is as artificial as their message.

So they object to being called pussyfoots in the pulpit . . . but what other description is appropriate?

How about Ecclesiastical Iscariots? After all, while their sellout isn't for thirty pieces of silver in a bag, it's for thousands of rand notes in the collection plate every Sunday from their comfortable white congregations.

# BOGEYMEN RIDE INTO BRYANSTON

*The antiapartheid Progressives were bidding to re-place the conservative United Party as the official op-position in the all-white parliament. Bryanston is one of the more affluent white suburbs of Johannesburg.*

All the world sympathizes with South Africa's nonvoters, but the South African voter also deserves some sympathy—no other voter in the world has his intelligence insulted so often and so systematically through appeals to the lowest human in-stincts.

In electoral politics there are two ways of getting sup-port: you either put forward well-reasoned policies in a call to the common sense of people, or you play on their basest instincts of fear, selfishness, and prejudice.

Here in South Africa the latter course has long proved

the most successful—the formula being to regard the voter as a total idiot, then to scare the hell out of him. The candidate who scares the voter most convincingly wins the election.

Now in Bryanston, near Johannesburg, where there is a by-election between the Progressives and the United Party, the U.P. has brought in some classical bogeymen, the main one being the Black Danger—better known through its Afrikaans appellation Swart Gevaar.

A pamphlet sent through the constituency implies that the Progs stand for black domination in South Africa, adding, rather guiltily, that "this is a plain fact, having nothing to do with Black Danger propaganda." Now how can a Black Danger pamphlet have nothing to do with Black Danger propaganda? Clearly the object of the pamphlet is to scare the Bryanston voters with Black Danger propaganda, and Black Danger is at least a first cousin of Swart Gevaar. . . .

The pamphlet then goes unintentionally into pure comedy. It says: "The United Party boldly advocates that black and white must cooperate together politically." Along separate lines, of course, and if anyone can explain how people can cooperate separately it would be appreciated. But wait, there is more of this hilarious stuff. How's this, for instance: "The party holds that South Africa is a country of human diversity . . ." Why not go further and boldly hold that water is wet, that ice is cold, and that fire is hot? Following this unequivocal assertion about human diversity, the pamphlet then suggests that a racial form of federation "will achieve political cooperation among our rich diversity of people" on what is described as "a firm foundation of own political power for each of the ethnocultural groups in our country."

Ethnocultural groups? Would you like your daughter to marry an ethnocultural group?

After twenty-seven years of double-talk in opposition, the United Party has brought the art to a peak. Consider this gem from party leader Graaff:

"The United Party is not moving to the right nor to the left, but forward!" And finally: "The United Party is a party of radical conservatism!"

Radical conservatism indeed! Liberal totalitarianism. Democratic dictatorship. Communist capitalism. Sick health. Dry wet. Gobbledegookityzookaboowoopazang.

Pity the poor voter who tries to decipher all these signals, which anyway are no longer necessary. Most of the all-white electorate knows by now that the real electoral argument among whites is basically between those who wish to resist black rights through open or disguised discrimination and those who do not.

Increasingly the more sophisticated urban voters, still a regrettable minority, are perceiving that no sound change to democracy can be too fast and that the conservative parties with their various blueprints for "reform" are moving too slowly for the country's safety.

In other words, if we want to avoid black panthers we have to stop supporting white tortoises.

# DEATH
# OF A DETAINEE

*August 1976 marked the first major reaction among
blacks to the death of a detainee, and this led to publication of the facts about others who had died in security police custody.*

Mapetla Mohapi, whose
writing reflected the viewpoint of the Black Consciousness Movement, graduated from Turfloop with a degree
in social science. Aged twenty-eight, he produced articles reasoned in tone, which evidenced a keen intellect.

He had a good sense of humor and a philosophical
readiness to tolerate petty harassment by the authorities, who kept threatening to evict him and his wife,
Nohle, and their two small children from their house
in the township—because of his articles.

But it was something else that stopped the articles—

some months ago Mapetla was banned, then seven weeks ago he was imprisoned without trial. Or "detained," to use our quaintly delicate word for this medieval action.

But his imprisonment didn't get him down, judging by two letters he smuggled out to Nohle. He had been detained before, for 180 days, and had experienced the torture of protracted solitary confinement. He was essentially a survivalist who lived for a cause, and like most detainees he knew more about the inside of prisons than about the insides of court buildings, since he'd never been charged with any crime.

Then late the other night I had a phone call from Steve Biko to convey the news that Mapetla had died suddenly in prison. Someone listening to our conversation uttered a high-pitched cackling laugh, and thereafter kept phoning Biko and me at all hours of the same night to repeat this performance.

It stopped only after I told the caller that every time he telephoned I would telephone his superior, to wake him up as well, so that we could all stay awake together. After his next call, at 3:30 A.M., I telephoned the regional head of the security police to tell him of this arrangement, and the mystery calls stopped immediately.

The death of Mapetla Mohapi, allegedly by hanging himself in his cell, drove me to look up the numbers of persons known to have died in detention in this country. Here is the list, followed in each case with the cause of death officially given by their captors:

1. L. NGUDLE died in Pretoria on September 5, 1963 (suicide by hanging)
2. B. MERHOPE died in Worcester on September 19, 1963 (causes undisclosed)
3. J. TYITYA died in Port Elizabeth on January 24, 1964 (suicide by hanging)
4. S. SALOOJEE died in Johannesburg on September 9, 1964 (fell seven floors during interrogation)
5. P. HOYE died in the Transkei on May 7, 1965 (natural causes)
6. N. GAGA died in the Transkei on May 8, 1965 (natural causes)
7. J. HAMAKWAYO died in Pretoria in 1966 (suicide by hanging)
8. H. SHONYEKA died in Pretoria on October 9, 1966 (suicide by hanging)
9. L. LEONG PIN died in Pretoria on November 19, 1966 (suicide by hanging)
10. A. AH YAN died in Pretoria on January 5, 1967 (suicide by hanging)
11. A. MADIBA died in an undisclosed prison on September 9, 1967 (suicide by hanging)
12. J. TUBAKWE died in Pretoria on September 11, 1968 (suicide by hanging)
13. AN UNNAMED PERSON died in an undisclosed place on an undisclosed date in 1968 (death disclosed in parliament on January 28, 1969)
14. N. NKGOATHE died in Pretoria on February 4, 1969 (slipped in shower)

15. S. MODIPANE died in prison on February 28, 1969 (slipped in shower)
16. J. LENKOE died in Pretoria on March 10, 1969 (suicide by hanging)
17. C. MAYEKISO died in Port Elizabeth on June 17, 1969 (suicide)
18. J. MONAKGOTLA died in Pretoria on September 10, 1969 (thrombosis)
19. IMAM A. HARON died in Cape Town on September 27, 1969 (fell down stairs)
20. M. CUTHSELA died in an undisclosed prison on January 21, 1971 (natural causes)
21. A. TIMOL died in Johannesburg on October 27, 1971 (leaped from tenth-floor window during interrogation)
22. J. MDLULI died in Durban on March 19, 1976 (causes later "disclosed")
23. M. MOHAPI died in Kei Road on August 5, 1976 (suicide by hanging)

The South African government, usually so ready to appoint commissions of inquiry into so many less important things, should appoint a commission of inquiry into why so many political detainees in this country are dying violent deaths while in security police custody.

This would be in everybody's interest, because in matters political it is not unknown for today's prisoners to be tomorrow's rulers.

And vice versa.

# REMEMBER THIS
# NAME WELL

*Steve Biko was imprisoned without trial four times, and this article related to the first of these four detentions. The idea was to try to prevent any assault on him, and in fact he wasn't assaulted until his final imprisonment in 1977, when he died after a severe beating.*

Almost a year ago I went to Minister J. T. Kruger and said that as serious urban violence seemed in prospect it would be sensible of the government to allow natural black leadership to emerge for purposes of peaceful negotiation.

I spoke in particular of a young black leader, twenty-eight-year-old Stephen Biko, who for several years had been under restriction, and suggested that the minister should consider lifting Biko's banning orders and allowing him to exercise his considerable gifts of leadership, considering the massive array of laws that could be used against him if he acted illegally.

I said that as a journalist who had interviewed politicians not only here in South Africa but also in America, Canada, Britain, Germany, France, Italy, and Israel, I had not encountered any as gifted in intellect, personality, and human understanding as Steve Biko.

A former medical student who had to give up his studies when banned, he had turned to studying law by correspondence in the area to which he was restricted, King William's Town, and as so many who had met him had raved about this extraordinary man who seemed to have "disciples" all over the country, I decided to find out what was so special about him.

After getting to know him I visited him often, enjoying many stimulating discussions with him. With all the benefits of a white education, I couldn't match wits with this relatively young man. Initially there were several areas of disagreement between us, as I had long regarded the Black Consciousness Movement as a negative and retrogressive development with racial undertones. But with increased understanding of all it implied came the realization that in today's circumstances its validity could be neither rationally questioned nor fully comprehended by a nonblack.

The movement's adherents were impressively different from most blacks one encountered. They walked taller, were more confident, at ease, and articulate. Ironically for purveyors of Black Consciousness, their blackness was the easiest thing to forget about them. This was particularly so in Steve Biko's case, in that his personality and philosophy far transcended matters of race and color.

Those discussions were memorable. His first few remarks were invariably humorous ones in Xhosa, then he would switch to English. And what English! There is no member of parliament in this country who uses the language with more effective ease. And his Afrikaans isn't too bad either, as he has a deep interest in language—an attribute that usually goes with a deep interest in people.

I tried to convey to Minister Kruger what Steve Biko is really like and pointed out that apart from a traffic fine he has never been convicted of any offense. I assumed he had been banned for founding SASO and helping to launch the Black Consciousness Movement, although neither act was against any law, and gave it as my opinion that after Mandela and Sobukwe, Biko is the leader most highly regarded by the politically aware urban blacks—especially the youth.

I stated that my own interest in the matter was to try to help avoid a situation in which black frustration would give rise to mindless violence through lack of articulate leadership and said that as a father of five children I was concerned to help keep the peace.

My plea obviously fell on deaf ears, because several weeks later the restrictions on Steve Biko were actually increased. And now he has been detained.

I don't know where he is being held, nor do I know what they think he has done wrong.

By normal standards I am fairly conservative, not unduly naïve and not easily impressed by politicians. But I'll tell you one thing: Make a note of the name Steve Biko and remember it well. One way or another it will be writ large in the history of South Africa.

He is not the first potential prime minister to be imprisoned without trial in this country. But I hope they treat him well while he is in prison, because he has a remarkable memory.

And so have his friends.

# TIME WAITS FOR NO CAUCUS

*In September 1976 there was a sense of crisis in South Africa, with violence in the townships flaring in a pattern that was to become familiar over the next decade. Yet the Vorster government retreated into its own party councils and appeared to have no grasp of the extent of black anger.*

Ten years have now passed since Mr. B. J. Vorster became prime minister, and in these ten years he has been generously indulged by the South African people, many of whom have recognized that an Afrikaner Nationalist leader has to function within the confines of his own narrow elite to retain the support of his party's caucus.

Over the past two weeks this indulgence has been stretched to the limit. Despite continuous uproar in the townships the whole country has been expected to wait with bated breath to learn its fate, while he has pondered this fate not with the nation's representatives but with the four provincial congresses and the caucus of his party.

We've all gone along with this little game for so many years that he probably believes a delay of a week or two is neither here nor there. But these days it is very much here. Time waits for no caucus, and in only three months there has been a decided shift in the sources of political power in this country.

It is no longer true that South Africa's future is entirely ordainable by the hierarchy of the Afrikaner Nationalist Party.

It's all very well for Mr. Vorster to go through the motions of party consultation as if his followers are the only people with power in this country today, but it is alarming to discover that he actually believes this. It means he is not simply playing the game according to the myth of government invincibility—he is taken in by it himself.

This sort of thing happens to people who move in restricted circles. If all your social and political engagements are with Afrikaner Nationalists; if enough schoolchildren pin flowers on your lapel; if party crowds keep surging to their feet to sing "Lank Mag Hy Lewe"; and if your colleagues award you enough tributes, honors, and citations, you can lose so much perspective that you regard the attitude of such people as representative of national reality.

Mr. Vorster's loss of perspective is serious. He recently remarked that an executive president in South

Africa would need to be in close touch with parliament. This suggests that he regards the present parliament as realistically representative of the South African nation—an astonishing proposition in these days.

After all, the assent of the present parliament means no more than the assent of the Afrikaner Nationalist Party, and that represents only one-twelfth of the people of this country. And as all policy is directed by the Broederbond, such representation actually comes down to a mere handful.

There is a section of the nation—the whites. There is a section of that section—the Afrikaners. There is a section of that section—the Afrikaner Nationalists. There is a section of that section—the Broederbond. So Mr. Vorster represents a section of a section of a section of a section of the nation.

This section is crippled by an emotional refusal to confront the reality of arithmetic in South Africa, and to remind them that there are more than 25 million black South Africans is as offensive to them as it would be to place a dead polecat on the dinner table at a formal banquet.

Mr. Vorster and his colleagues don't want to talk about such things because they don't want to think about such things. Hence their perpetual ignoring of the obvious and their regular resort to the comforting explanation.

Take the township riots. These are not seen as manifestations of black anger, but are ascribed to "agitators" and "Communists," enabling the government to prolong the myth that the militancy of the minority is rejected by the black majority.

The time has come for them to consult the real leaders of the blacks.

They won't be hard to find.

They're all in prison.

# KISSINGER AND
# THE CROCODILE

*It suited the interests of South Africa and the United States to pressure Ian Smith of Rhodesia into negotiations with black leaders in what was to become Zimbabwe, and such pressure duly followed the visit of Dr. Henry Kissinger to South Africa for talks with Vorster and his colleagues.*

Winston Churchill, commenting on the readiness of Chamberlain and others to make territorial concessions to Hitler in Europe, said: "Each one thinks that if he feeds the crocodile, the crocodile will eat him last."

If today's crocodile is black majority rule, today's most motivated crocodile feeder is Premier B. J. Vorster. With the help of Dr. Henry Kissinger he is preparing two succulent chunks of meat for the croc—Zimbabwe (nee Rhodesia) and Namibia (nee South West Africa).

So much for today. But what of the main item on tomorrow's menu, Azania (nee South Africa)? Mr. Vorster seeks to divert attention from this item with a few cutlets from the deep freeze. Next month the Transkei is on the menu, to be followed by Ciskei, Venda, and other "homelands" still to be "consolidated."

But these chops are too small for the croc. They are mere morsels, and if there's anything a hungry croc hates it is an unconsolidated chop.

And even if these Bantustan chops were fed to the croc, what then? Does our Prime Feeder really think the croc will waggle its tail gratefully and slither back into the water to "develop along its own lines?"

The Vorster-Kissinger initiative on Rhodesia is fine. The sooner Smith is forced to accept reality and the white Rhodesians learn to live with black majority rule the sooner there will be peace in that country. But it is strangely inconsistent to assume that such adjustments to reality need not extend south of the Limpopo River.

South Africa's own policies were not on the Kissinger agenda, and Dr. Kissinger's own schedule in this country included talks with more than two dozen leaders of various kinds—not one of whom represented the black majority.

Whatever benefits may flow from Dr. Kissinger's visit in respect of Rhodesia, the Americans should not be surprised if the result of the visit is anti-American reaction among blacks. They saw him come here and fail to demand to speak to Mandela, Sobukwe, Biko, Pityana, Mbeki, and Rachidi.

This oversight will make the crocodile hungrier, homeland cutlets notwithstanding, when the Prime Feeder runs out of party-approved meat.

# MY TURN TO SERVE

*Harold Levy, barrister extraordinary, managed on the barest technicality to get the prison sentence on me reversed in one of the higher courts not yet dominated by progovernment judges. The technicality was that documentary process had been served by the wrong official for purposes of trial and sentence.*

For more than a year I've been engaged in a grim legal tennis match with the head of the security police, General Michiel Geldenhuys, and yesterday the supreme court overruled a magistrate's sentence on me of six months' imprisonment.

The government is taking the case higher, to the Appeal Court, but before it does so certain aspects of the matter can now be discussed, including the year-long process General Geldenhuys initiated to get me into prison. He must be a disappointed man this morning, but I have further bad news for him, because in terms of our litigational tennis match he has just dropped his service and it's my turn to serve.

Security police officers don't really understand law, which is why their record of getting people into prison via the courts is so unsuccessful, and why they have to resort so often to detention without trial. But General Geldenhuys has now got himself involved in this case, so he better start brushing up his return of serve.

The general will recall that this whole business started with certain allegations I made against one of his security police officers, and that instead of taking action against this man he took action against me. But now that this action has failed, it's time for his man to face the music.

On the evening of September 21, 1964, Warrant Officer Gerhardus Hattingh lurked in the shadows of the Hogsback Inn, a mountain resort in the Eastern Cape. Parked in the hotel grounds was a car he had followed all afternoon, a car belonging to the author Alan Paton, and that night while the Patons were asleep inside the hotel Hattingh took several stones the size of a melon and smashed in the windows.

Another officer of the security police at the time was Warrant Officer Donald John Card, to whom Hattingh boasted of his feat. Card was shaken to hear what Hattingh had done, but remained silent out of loyalty to a colleague. Card later left the security police, and he and I became friends.

Then a year ago I complained to the authorities about Hattingh's bullying propensities in connection with another matter, and only after further probing spoke of the Paton incident, of which Card had told me when I asked him what sort of person Hattingh was.

I refused to name Card as the witness, but when I was subpoenaed by order of General Geldenhuys, Card insisted and stated his readiness to testify.

The time has now come to use this evidence and proceed against Hattingh, and to get General Geldenhuys moving in connection with this case, here is some further information for him. It concerns law, and particularly the Law of Evidence, about which the general obviously knows little.

In an interview published in the Johannesburg *Sunday Express* of October 31 this year, General Geldenhuys said Card's evidence against Hattingh would be inadmissible because it was hearsay. But General Geldenhuys is wrong, as any lawyer could tell him.

Hearsay evidence is indirect and inadmissible as testimony of what a second party is reported to have perceived, but Card's evidence is both direct and admissible because it is a first-person account of what Card himself heard, namely Hattingh's statement to him.

There are two further legal points that may be confusing General Geldenhuys. One is the inadmissibility of a confession made to a peace officer. But this does not apply as between one policeman and another, and Hattingh's statement being not a confession but an admission constitutes evidence that is both direct and admissible.

Finally, the action is not invalid through praescriptio

longi temporis, because twelve of the twenty years have elapsed.

So there you are, General Geldenhuys. You said you required evidence against Hattingh and now you've got it. You have a witness who is prepared to testify, whose evidence is both direct and admissible, and there is supportive circumstantial evidence from security police records regarding Hattingh's whereabouts at the time.

By the way, if you now still decline to prosecute, this will not help Hattingh, because Alan Paton will institute a private prosecution and your man will end up in court in any case.

And following criminal proceedings there will probably be civil proceedings as well, because interest on the money Mr. Paton had to pay for repairs to his vandalized car can now be calculated over all the years since the crime was committed.

Then there is the question of legal costs all around, so one way and another Mr. Hattingh's little caper on that fateful evening could end up costing him a packet.

But that's justice, isn't it, General Geldenhuys? And justice is what we're after, isn't it?

In Hattingh's case, whether he wants it or not, he's going to get it.

I've had my turn in the dock. Now it's his turn.

# TELL THEM
# TO STOP

*Attacks on the homes and families of dissidents were increasingly being carried out by security police or their associates as members of self-appointed white vigilante groups, and these attacks clearly had the tacit approval of the government.*

The government should condemn all acts of vandalism, harassment, and terrorism against critics of apartheid. If it doesn't, the present spate of injuries and deaths among dissidents will continue.

Our rulers must know there is a certain mentality that takes its cue from above and assumes in the absence of public condemnation that there is an official green light of approval for such attacks.

Members of the Christian Institute such as Theo Kotze have recently suffered such attacks in the so-called Scorpio incidents, and there are many examples of which the public are well aware. What they are not aware of, however, is whether the government wants these attacks to stop.

Far from condemning such actions, Prime Minister Vorster has said things that give the opposite impression. He threatens to let "his boys" loose among dissenters, and after criminal assaults by police against student demonstrators, he says that if the police had acted differently he would have been disappointed in them.

What sort of talk is this from a prime minister in a country already full of dangerous tensions? It can encourage more than assault. There are still unanswered questions about the deaths of detainees while under "interrogation," such as Imam Haron of Cape Town.

Four months ago I listed in this column twenty-three names of detainees who have died violently in custody, and in these four months that list has grown to a shocking thirty-one.

Here are the names of the new victims, with the official reasons for their deaths given in parentheses:

24. L. MAZWEMBE died in Cape Town on September 2, 1976 (suicide by hanging)
25. D. MBATHA died in an undisclosed prison on September 25, 1976 (suicide by hanging)
26. E. MZOLO died in Johannesburg on October 1, 1976 (no details given)
27. W. TSHWANE died on October 14, 1976 (no details given)

28. E. MAMASILA died on November 18, 1976 (no details given)
29. T. MOSALA died in Butterworth on November 26, 1976 (no details given)
30. W. TSHAZIBANE died on December 11, 1976 (no details given)
31. G. BOTHA died in Port Elizabeth on December 14, 1976 (fell down stairwell)

As pointed out before in this column, the government should immediately appoint a judicial commission of inquiry into these deaths, and take urgent steps to prevent any more.

# NO TIME
# FOR TRUCES

*In spite of growing black anger in the townships, white politicians on both sides were acting as though theirs was a genuine parliament, deserving of rules and customs as observed in normal parliaments of democratic countries.*

As Christmas dawns, so does the traditional political truce in this country in terms of which white politicians observe a verbal cease-fire until parliament reconvenes in the new year. Like many South African traditions it is a bad one, suggesting normality where there is abnormality, as if political differences here were marginal matters of administrative dispute rather than deep determinants of misery for millions.

Let the democracies have Christmas truces. We are not in such mild and civilized circumstances. The things happening in South Africa cannot be suspended from consideration while Yuletide turkeys are carved and festive glasses clinked.

It is sickening when privileged politicians enjoy comfortable rules about debate among their right honorable selves while the victims of such debate may not even take part in it, or even object too strongly about it without being thrown into prison.

There is still no inquiry instituted into the growing number of deaths in detention, and there is no time for truces while this shocking issue is unresolved. If a government assumes the right to imprison people without trial, it has an extra obligation to protect them during such imprisonment—from everything including their own suicidal tendencies if in fact these exist.

If such protection is not provided, the government must take the blame for such deaths as have occurred, and ensure that others will not occur.

So far we have not even heard a public expression of concern about them from any member of the government, and while this issue remains unresolved let all concerned have a thoughtful rather than a merry Christmas.

# HOW TO
# MAKE BILTONG

*Government annoyance over several recent articles in this series was by now barely contained, and I felt it advisable to lie low for a time. Hence this parody on the style of the South African prose writer Herman Charles Bosman, noted for his chronicles of rustic scenes and national customs.*

One of the main culinary achievements of South Africa is well-made biltong, and, figuratively speaking, I recently sat at the feet of one of the masters of the art, Jacobus Nel Van Wyk, who accompanied me from the Eastern Cape to Pretoria. With more than a thousand miles there and back to devote to conversation, I had a rare opportunity to learn the intricacies of the art.

Those who think biltong is merely dried meat are fools. Hearing Oom Jac on the subject is like hearing Bach on the art of fugue. I broached the subject near

Cathcart, and it took him to past Bloemfontein before the finer points were dealt with.

But it was as we approached the Orange River area that his nostrils started to quiver like those of an old warhorse who smells gunpowder. He observed that we were now approaching the best biltong country, in terms of the right sort of grazing, because the grazing determines the texture of the meat. Then he was off into detailed prescription, and I hereby pass on his advice.

The first thing is to choose your meat, he says with his eyes closed as if in prayer. Biltong can of course be made from the meat of a variety of animals, including springbok, gemsbok, kudu, bushbuck, and various types of birds such as ostrich. Oom Jac once knew of an unprincipled man who made biltong from donkey, and he regards this man as an enemy of South Africa.

Without question the best biltong is from beef, he says, and his eyes get a faraway look as he goes into the history of biltong, for he is a man who believes in beginning at the beginning. Oom Jac says the word came from an old trekboer who said of the thick strips of dried meat he was preparing that each resembled a "bul se tong," a bull's tongue.

He does not deign to respond to my suggestion that the word has a Malay sound and might have come from the Cape Malay slaves who gave us such words as "blatjang." Bul se tong, he repeats firmly.

For only the best biltong, says Oom Jac, a disciplined formula must be followed, starting with choice of the best beef. The animal must be in good condition and well grazed in a good stock area, preferably in the regions of Burgersdorp, Aliwal North or Queenstown, where the grass is sweetest.

After slaughtering, allow the meat to cool overnight, then cut on the membrane along the grain from the haunches on either side of the spine strips measuring about 30 centimeters by 7 centimeters.

Then take the skin of the ox, wash it thoroughly, and let it dry out almost completely. When it is almost dry, spread it out with the hair side down and salt the upper side with coarse salt. Salt the meat strips as well, then wrap them in the salted hide and leave this folded hide in a cool dark room for four days and four nights.

This sounds so biblical that I interject: "You mean four days, Oom Jac?"

He replies emphatically: "Four days and four nights."

After the fourth night, he continues, prepare a bucketful of water and vinegar, fourteen parts water to one part vinegar, in which is dissolved a half-kilogram of brown sugar, then dip the strips of meat into this solution and hang them up to dry.

At this point Oom Jac fixes you with a fierce look and says in a dreadful voice: "Use only stainless steel hooks!"

The strips must then be hung in a well-ventilated room and left "for eight days and eight nights."

Oom Jac has no time for people who hang biltong in the sun to dry. The meat must dry naturally, he says, not from the direct heat of the sun. He regards people who hang meat in the sun as worse than Communists.

The ideal condition of biltong, he says, is that the outside must be dry but the inside slightly moist. And it should always be cut against the grain, not with it.

With a stainless steel knife? Ja, natuurlik!

Passionate as he is about his art, Oom Jac is modest about his own place in the biltong-making hierarchy. When I asked him if there was a greater biltong maker in all South Africa than himself he grew thoughtful, peering into the distance as he considered the question.

Finally he replied, with a kind of reverence:

"Manie Venter of Zastron."

# OF WEAPONS
# AND WARRIORS

*Police Minister Kruger was constantly claiming that township violence was Communist-directed, and during a debate in parliament he produced a Soviet machine gun he said his men had found in Soweto, in support of his contention. He had obviously learned to strip and reassemble it, which he did several times during his speech with inordinate satisfaction.*

Watching the opening salvoes of this year's session of parliament was like seeing the rescreening of an old film one has seen many times before, with the opposition vainly trying to widen the debate to broader national issues and the government relentlessly forcing the debate back into the limits of white party politics.

About the only departure from previous scripts was the production by Minister Kruger of a gun found in Soweto, which he alternately brandished and caressed, clearly enjoying the experience. Handling any weapon of war is such a new experience for members of the governing party that they openly relish the novelty.

But according to opposition members, who have actually fought in a war, it is a thing to be avoided because its reality is so horribly different from its macho image in the eyes of armchair militarists and party congress patriots.

Some members of the government have had paramilitary experience, of course. Mr. Vorster was a "general" in the OssewaBrandwag, although this organization was in action against our own bridges and railway lines rather then enemy forces. Still, the experience of some sort of paramilitary life might stand him in good stead if we enter an era in which politicians become involved with the consequences of their policies.

It would make a lot of sense from now on to give our most vocal patriots the opportunity to serve in the front lines in the border areas now coming under challenge from guerrillas of the outlawed black organizations.

They are the ones most ready to proclaim that whites will fight "to the last drop of blood." Let them be the first to demonstrate it, instead of sending young men up to the borders and into Angola to do the fighting their speeches precipitate.

Training needn't be a problem. Members of the opposition with service experience would surely be willing to train members of the governing party to face combat conditions.

Perhaps Mr. Kruger's newly acquired expertise in assembling a machine gun should not be dismissed too lightly.

He may yet need it.

# LOCKED
# IN THE LAAGER

*The Afrikaans newspapers seldom addressed the real
issues of apartheid, usually taking refuge in coverage
of peripheral matters, and when an Afrikaner businessman was mildly critical of state policy they chose
to cover Vorster's put-down of the man rather than
the issue he had raised.*

Afrikaner chauvinism is
becoming as much of a danger to itself as to the major
part of the nation, and today there is probably no iden-
tifiable group in the world as cut off from the think-
ing and attitudes of their fellow countrymen as this
group is.

Recently the Afrikaans-language newspaper, *Rapport*,
commenting on the mild clash between businessman
Theo Wassenaar and Premier Vorster, said that when
Afrikaner opposes Afrikaner it is a case of "bul teen

bul." About all I would agree with in this context is the appropriateness of the word "bull."

This sort of precious self-consciousness is what prevents significant debate within Afrikaner Nationalist ranks, because if you really analyze what happens in such "confrontations" you find it is nothing like a case of one bull locking horns with another.

Admittedly there is much snorting and pawing of the ground, but what happens is that the bulls charge past each other. They don't actually come into conflict. Instead of dealing with the mildly made points of Mr. Wassenaar, Mr. Vorster appealed to the emotions of the Volk for solidarity.

Within this emotional laager you never deal with real issues. You win an argument not with a logical disputation of facts but by appealing for an emotional endorsement from the group, and this endorsement is gained by rallying the chiefs and headmen of this particular tribe on grounds relating to their hierarchical standing and survival.

The result is that no one within the Afrikaner Nationalist establishment ever publicly challenges it and survives within it. Yet the myth about vigorous individualists persists, so that the mildest murmurings can be likened to a head-on clash between two bulls!

It is all part of the self-deception endemic to a group that refuses to see itself in terms other than its own. All those statues, monuments, and memorials, and all those tunnels, dams, and airports they keep putting their own names on, give them an exaggerated impression of their influence and power.

And a dangerous illusion of their permanence as rulers.

We've all heard of those who can't see the forest for the trees. But in our context what could be more foolish than a ruling group that can't see the Nation for the Volk?

# THOROUGHLY
# MISUNDERSTOOD
# EMILY

*Government speeches attacking Helen Suzman
reached a crescendo at this time, and this article was
an attempt to help her through invoking one of the
favorite heroines of Afrikaner Nationalists.*

The name of Emily Hob-
house is revered by Afrikaners, and with reason. She
was the remarkable Englishwoman who pleaded the
Boer cause in Britain and came to South Africa to help
the Boer women and children in the concentration
camps during the Anglo-Boer War at the turn of the
century.

Grateful Afrikanerdom has never forgotten her. She
is buried at the Vrouemonument in Bloemfontein and
her name is perpetuated—there is a town and a modern

submarine named after her, not to mention several branches of the governing party.

But most of her admirers in this country don't understand what she really stood for, and would be shocked if they did.

An attractive Cornishwoman in her thirties when she adopted the Boer cause, she was of a leading Liberal family and became hated in Britain for championing the Boer underdogs by campaigning against the war.

At a stage of history obsessed with militaristic patriotism she was antiwar in principle, which makes the naming of that submarine one of the supreme ironies of how she is commemorated here. But there are other ironies.

She put humanity above patriotism, and people above flags and anthems. She stood up for the oppressed and repeatedly defied her own government, scorning accusations of treason and treachery, and she was deeply opposed to racism.

In fact, she had a lot in common with Helen Suzman.

Soon after the formation of the Afrikaner Nationalist Party she took issue with the first emerging signs of apartheid mentality among the Volk, writing as early as 1924: "Personally I believe segregation by race, color or class the wrong policy and one which can only lead to discontent and ultimate disaster." She added that she had not labored for the Boer cause only to see the Boers inflict on others the injustices that had been inflicted on themselves.

In her old age she was still writing sharp letters to Pretoria. She was against monuments and chauvinism, and warned: "Some day Pretoria too will be as Zimbabwe, as Nineveh and Thebes . . . and perhaps the bombs of aviators will bring it about." She said the most fitting monument Afrikaners could erect in memory of their dead would be a spirit of reconciliation.

In her speech drafted for the opening of the Vrouemonument she said: "To harbor hate is fatal to your self-development. It makes a flaw, for hatred, like rust, eats into the soul of a nation as of an individual. Instead forgive the rich who were greedy of more riches, the statesmen who could not guide affairs, the bad generalship that warred on weaklings and babes—forgive, for only so can you rise to full nobility of character and a broad national life."

Emily Hobhouse believed no lasting benefit could be gained at the expense of others, and that only by striving to gain for others the rights we wish for ourselves can there be real reconciliation.

If Emily Hobhouse were alive today she would assuredly be a member of the Black Sash, and this government would have no more furious foe. She would be demonstrating against conditions in Soweto, she would be obstructing the bulldozers demolishing squatters' homes at Crossroads, she would be raising hell over the list of deaths in detention.

In all probability she would be banned.

# OPEN LETTER TO VORSTER

*During March 1977 Prime Minister Vorster repeatedly threatened to crack down further on the press with additional laws curbing criticism of state policy, and he whipped up white feeling against the few independent newspapers by labeling them disloyal and unpatriotic.*

Prime Minister Vorster,

It is said that your great ambition is to be bracketed in history with the Afrikaner Nationalist leaders of the past—Malan, Strijdom, and Verwoerd.

You will, Mr. Vorster, you will.

Your party took over, in 1948, a country that was popular abroad. A survey conducted in the previous year showed that 87 percent of all emigrants from war-torn Europe chose South Africa as their intended home—until your party stopped them.

South Africa's good name in those days was due to
the reputation of General Smuts (whom you abhorred),
participation in the Allied cause in World War II (which
you opposed), our role in world politics (which you reversed), and our achievements in international sport
(which you wrecked).

In 1948 South Africa was poised for one of the greatest forward surges any modern country could hope for,
with the most favorable position in the world to which
any small country could aspire, and the enlightened lib-
eralism of that towering genius, Jan Hofmeyr, had
opened the door and shown the way to a future set
against racism.

Then your party took over. You took this country
with all its assets and reversed its entire course. You
threw away the assets and built up the liabilities.

First you turned the immigrant ships back, with all
the skills and dedication they would have brought. Then
you foreswore the entire six-year war against dictatorship and tyranny, releasing pro-Nazis and saboteurs and
fascists from South African prisons.

You brought in apartheid. You painted racial signs on
park benches, post offices, railway carriages, and public
entrances, passing one unjust racial law after another.

You gained votes by turning whites against blacks, by
playing on white fears, by exploiting white greed. Then,
as if the black majority were not enough enemies for
the whites of South Africa, you began to provoke into
being what is today literally a world of sworn enemies.

Of your own role in all this, Mr. Vorster, it can be

said that when you make mistakes you make them big. Remember the D'Oliveira affair? For a few ragged cheers at a party congress you barred a touring British sports team because one of its members, Basil D'Oliveira, was of mixed race, and that action began the death process for this country's participation in international sport while your policies prevail.

Now you propose a Newspaper Bill, to add to all the existing dozens of publication restrictions and to tame what is left of an independent press in this country.

It is many years since the South African press could indulge in the old motto: Publish and be damned.

So go ahead and indulge your stated intention to tame us further.

Legislate and be damned.

# OPEN LETTER TO
# KRUGER

*By now Police Minister Kruger was joining in Vor-
ster's threats against the press and was stepping up
detention of dissidents, holding many of them in solitary confinement. Government speakers claimed such
actions were necessary "to safeguard Christian values
in South Africa."*

Minister Kruger,

As minister of justice, police, and prisons you bear a
heavy responsibility for the state of justice, police, and
prisons in South Africa at this time.

It is said that justice must not only be done but must
be seen to be done. Too often in this country it has
neither been done nor been seen to be done.

Take the particular anguish of persons not only imprisoned without trial but held in solitary confinement.
Psychologists state with wide authority that solitary

confinement is in itself a severe form of torture and can often be more harmful than actual physical assault.

Being kept alone in a small, confined space, being deprived of human contact with friends and loved ones, not knowing what one's captors might do—these things have driven people mad.

How can you and your colleagues in the cabinet claim, as you so often do, that you follow Christian principles? If you were innocent of crime, would it be fair to imprison you? And in imprisoning innocent persons and holding them in solitary confinement, are you doing to them what you would have them do unto you?

You might reply that innocent persons are not imprisoned without trial, but of course they are. I can prove it, and I could call you, Mr. Kruger, as a witness in two capacities to prove it. First, as a lawyer, you know that a man should be presumed innocent until proved guilty, and that if not proved guilty in a proper court of law he must be presumed innocent. Second, as a self-described Christian you know that one of the worst offenses against the Christian ethic is bearing false witness against your neighbor.

Is there any more blatant bearing of false witness than the imprisonment of a person without the taking and testing of testimony? It is the branding of an innocent in the eyes of all society without proof of the absence of that innocence.

Finally, as ultimate head of the security police you know how often people are imprisoned here on the untested word of a security police officer or his informer, who has a financial interest in providing damaging reports about dissidents. Indeed, the very nature of the work of an informer is such that it could fairly be described as seeking payment for bearing false witness.

Furthermore, there is a final, practical reason why you should prevail on your cabinet colleagues to end solitary confinement and imprisonment without trial: A future South African government may enact retrospective legislation to bring to justice officials who at any time in the past were responsible for such offenses against humanity.

# OPEN LETTER TO
# M. C. BOTHA

*One of the leading figures in the government most hated by young blacks was M. C. Botha, whose decree that they had to be taught through the medium of Afrikaans had triggered off the Soweto riots.*

Minister Botha,

As Minister of Bantu Administration and Education, does it ever strike you that your department, and the very name of your department, is a sociopolitical oddity?

Just repeat to yourself the words: "Department of Bantu Administration and Education . . ."

Only someone deeply ignorant of the black language could apply the word "Bantu" (actually, more correctly "aBantu" meaning "people") to the indigenous African group in this country. But the idea behind it is even more bizarre.

There is something essentially weird in the concept of a government department dealing with the administration and education of a group defined legally by its skin pigmentation.

If such eccentric grounds for differentiation must exist, why stop there? Why not have special departments legislating for left-handed people and redheads and short people and tall people?

If physical appearance is the main determinant, why not a plethora of government portfolios for fat people, thin people, ugly people, and beautiful people?

As for your department's leading personnel, does it not seem strange to you that the three top officials in a department with responsibility for blacks—yourself, Mr. Raubenheimer, and Dr. Treurnicht—are all noted for your extreme views on race? It's rather like putting Alan Paton, Beyers Naude, and Helen Suzman in charge of Broederbond.

Then let us recall the official reasons given for the setting up of the Department of Bantu Education by its creator, Dr. Hendrik Verwoerd, who explained that it was necessary to train blacks for different expectations of life because in terms of apartheid policy there was no place for blacks in the white community "above certain forms of labor."

It was emphasized that to provide blacks with the same standard of education as whites would be to create "wrong expectations" among them.

The sooner we move away from this kind of craziness the better, and a good way to start would be to abolish your department.

The only race we should concern ourselves with in South Africa should be the human race.

# OPEN LETTER TO
# PIK BOTHA

*South Africans love to bestow nicknames that represent opposites of physical characteristics. Thus Roelof Botha, foreign minister, who was big and tall, was nicknamed "Pik," which in Afrikaans means "tiny" or "peewee." Long rumored to be more liberal than his associates, he was nevertheless always ready to conform when whistled back to heel.*

Minister Botha,

As newly appointed minister of foreign affairs your key task will be to change the old plaint that the world hates us because our policies are misunderstood. You are now going to have to break the news to your cabinet colleagues that the world hates us because our policies are very well understood indeed.

Tell them also that the more apartheid is explained abroad, the more hostile the world will become toward it, and that if ever the West comes to a complete comprehension of what is going on here, far from the West supporting Pretoria against the Eastern bloc it will in fact join the East and the Third World against Pretoria.

Then, finally, that could mean economic sanctions being applied to this country as the only practical non-violent way the world can pressure this government to the negotiating table with the real leaders of the black majority.

Forget about strategic minerals, the Cape Sea Route, and all that stuff. The stakes are higher than these, and ultimately the West cannot afford to appear sympathetic to minority white racism here.

So yours is the toughest selling job there is—not the selling of apartheid to the world, but the selling of the idea to your cabinet colleagues that as far as racial discrimination is concerned the game is up.

The more they try to cling to now, the more they will lose later.

Right now a peaceful future for South Africa may well rest more on your personal persuasiveness than on anything else.

Good luck!

# OPEN LETTER TO
# P. W. BOTHA

*This article was to be republished in many newspapers, and students of Cape Town University had a framed version in blown-up type sent to Mr. Botha to ensure that he read it.*

Minister Botha,

You ask who will rejoice if your government is toppled?

You say that Moscow and Peking will rejoice, but who else?

Well, most of the people of this country will rejoice. Cape Town will rejoice. Johannesburg will rejoice. Durban will rejoice. Port Elizabeth, East London, and Pietermaritzburg will rejoice. Germiston, Springs, and Benoni will rejoice. Every major South African city, apart from Pretoria and Bloemfontein, will rejoice. Mdantsane will rejoice. Soweto will rejoice. Langa, New Brighton, and Guguletu will rejoice.

And outside the country, too. Nairobi will rejoice. Cairo will rejoice. Jerusalem, Tel Aviv, and Baghdad will rejoice. Algiers will rejoice. Lagos, Luanda, and Casablanca will rejoice. Marrakesh and Rabat and Addis Ababa will rejoice. Timbuktu will rejoice.

London, New York, Paris, Rome, Bonn, and Berlin will rejoice. Chicago, Los Angeles, San Francisco, Washington, Boston, New Orleans, and St. Louis will rejoice. Ottawa will rejoice. Toronto, Montreal, Quebec, Vancouver, and Winnipeg will rejoice.

Dublin and Belfast will rejoice. Glasgow, Edinburgh, and Aberdeen will rejoice. Bristol will rejoice. Cardiff and Swansea will rejoice. Birmingham, Manchester, and Leeds will rejoice.

Marseilles will rejoice. Bordeaux will rejoice. Amsterdam, The Hague, and Rotterdam will rejoice. Stockholm, Oslo, Copenhagen, and Helsinki will rejoice. Madrid will rejoice. Lisbon will rejoice. Milan, Naples, and Venice will rejoice. Vienna will rejoice. Athens will rejoice. Belgrade, Budapest, and Warsaw will rejoice.

Calcutta will rejoice. Bombay, Madras, New Delhi, and Karachi will rejoice. Bangkok will rejoice. Singapore, Hong Kong, and Jakarta will rejoice.

Sydney will rejoice. Melbourne will rejoice. Adelaide, Perth, and Brisbane will rejoice. Canberra will rejoice.

Auckland will rejoice. Wellington, Christchurch, and Dunedin will rejoice.

Can you be serious, Mr. Botha, when you ask who will rejoice when your government is toppled from power?

The whole bloody world will rejoice.

# LEGION OF
# THE BANNED

*Even as recently as April 1977 most white South Africans were ignorant of black politics and politicians, and few had heard of Steve Biko or his associates.*

Significant though events in the Eastern Cape have been in recent months, and well reported though they have been locally, people in the rest of the country know little about them.

This is due only partly to suppression of news, because even the newspapers not controlled by the governing party are generally locked into a white urban value system that accords little weight to events occurring outside that value system.

Recently in King William's Town one of the most interesting inquests in South African history was conducted—into the death of Mapetla Mohapi—making front-page news day after day in the region. Among the black crowds in and outside the courtroom were some of the most important personalities in black politics in this country.

Yet even in the neighboring city of Port Elizabeth not one of the three daily newspapers there carried prominent reports about this inquest. In fact, two of them ignored it utterly. The inquest has now been adjourned to later in the year.

So as far as most white South Africans are concerned it either never happened or is of minor significance.

Minor significance? One day South African schoolchildren will read about it in their history books!

Another important case now adjourned is the prosecution of Steve Biko—a case followed with interest by several major embassies, yet accorded barely a paragraph or two in most of the newspapers.

This at a time when even the most obscure white politician gets major coverage for any trivial statement, and when minor white civil servants are televised in excruciating detail on the most frivolous issues.

If we had real television in this country instead of a tame party-controlled service, one of our nationally best-known characters would be a dynamic twenty-eight-year-old woman with the personality of a cyclone. Slight in build but in nothing else, she is a medical doctor who is one of the heroines of the Black Consciousness Movement.

She is Dr. Mampela Ramphele, until last Thursday the head of Zanempilo Clinic near King William's Town, which was founded by young blacks who carry community self-help into rural black areas. She is one of two women particularly prominent in the movement, the other being Tenji Mtintso, recently banned after a long spell in solitary confinement.

Dr. Ramphele was detained last year for a long time before being released without accusation or explanation of any kind. Then suddenly last Thursday she was banned and banished to a remote place in the northern Transvaal, a thousand miles away.

And beyond the Eastern Cape, there was neither a report nor a ripple of interest. Not a white ripple, that is . . .

On the same day I was at a meeting of editors in Cape Town and heard some of them talking about the absence of black leadership.

Well, the fact that they don't know about black leaders explains why their leaders don't know about them either. In fact, most whites seldom hear about black leaders because most of the latter are banned, in prison, or underground, and that is yet another reason for white ignorance of the scale and scope of black political feeling in this country.

Dr. Ramphele, Tenji Mtintso, and Fatima Meer are as significant to blacks politically as Helen Suzman is to white parliamentary politics, as are Nelson Mandela, Robert Sobukwe, Steve Biko, Barney Pityana, Saths

Cooper, Strini Moodley, Mxolisi Mvovo, Hlaku Rachidi, Thami Zani, Malusi Mpumlwana, Dilize Mji, and Dr. Neville Alexander to most people in this country.

Although most of these belong to the "legion of the banned," they have high credibility in black politics and whites should be told about them and their thoughts and aims. In fact news of them should be given more prominence than news of white politicians, because they have so many more followers.

It is up to us, the journalists of South Africa, to do our job properly and keep the whole nation informed of significant news.

The white politicians may choose to wear blinders, but we don't have to.

# A SELF-LIBERATED
WOMAN

*Few whites knew much about banning, or about how
it is imposed and policed, and very few indeed actually knew a banned person or members of such a
person's family.*

$D$r. Mampela Ramphele,
aforementioned head of the Zanempilo Clinic and leading functionary of the Black Consciousness Movement,
has been doing a lot of traveling lately.

First she was served with a banning order, then ordered to be confined to a remote area of the country,
then put into a car and driven a thousand miles to Tza-
neen in the far north, in the custody of Warrant Officer
Gerhardus Hattingh also aforementioned.

But no sooner had Warrant Officer Hattingh delivered
her into exile and returned to his normal duty of watch-

147

ing Steve Biko and his colleagues back in King William's Town than I was receiving an invitation to breakfast at the clinic with the doughty doctor herself. Hard on the heels of Hattingh she had cadged a car and followed him all the way back to resume her duties at the clinic.

The breaking of a banning order is a serious business. You are not supposed to budge from your place of confinement (especially not to budge a thousand miles from it) nor to be with more than one person at a time. Yet here were several of us having a hilarious breakfast as we heard her story.

It seems that she had barely been delivered to the far north by the warrant officer when a careful scrutiny of her banning order revealed that her name was misspelled and the wrong identity number given, so she declared herself unbanned and came home to resume work.

She delivered a baby almost immediately, also a contravention of the ban since the birth of the child constituted a third person in the room and therefore an unlawful assembly.

And as the baby was black, her delivery of it probably constituted a contravention of the prohibition on furthering the aims and objects of black resistance.

Within a few days the ban was reimposed, this time using the correct spelling and identity number, and Warrant Officer Hattingh had another long drive to the remote north.

Apartheid costs taxpayers a lot of money, doesn't it?

# A PARODY FOR
# POLITICIANS

*With white parliamentary politics becoming increasingly irrelevant, the party most guilty of irrelevancy was the anachronistic United Party, which blundered on in disarray, getting in the way of the more serious contenders.*

The once-mighty United Party of Jan Smuts has dwindled since his death to a mere handful of members in the parliament it used to dominate with more than a hundred seats in its days as the government of the land.

But the saddest aspect of this decline has been the manner of it. It has been marked by compromise of principle, ambiguity of policy, desertion of ideals, and constant refusal to stand up to the Afrikaner Nationalists in their relentless pursuit of total apartheid.

This lackluster slide into oblivion has been presided

over by South Africa's only baronet, Sir De Villiers Graaff, who has led the party from one retreat to another, piling policy disaster onto policy disaster as his ranks of followers have been whittled down from election to election.

Today only Sir "Div" himself and his two main associates, Gray Hughes and the even more racist Theo Gerdener, are the recognizable remnant of the party.

The barely surviving rump of the party in Natal is entrusted to the amiable Warwick Webber. (Alas, poor Warwick, I knew him well, Horatio . . . )

So the story of the United Party since the 1948 election defeat is like an epic in reverse, and it seems that some Tennysonian lines are in order to record the erosion of its national congress luminaries from six hundred down to the final three of Div Graaff, Gray Hughes, and Theo Gerdener.

Here's an attempt:

### CHARGE OF THE LIGHTWEIGHT BRIGADE

Half a league, half a league, half a league
    onward
Into the wilderness rode the six hundred.

Votes to the right of them, votes to the left of
    them,
Votes through the midst of them, many seats
    squandered.

Led by the Baronet and his newfound cadet,
Into fresh folly yet—foolish five hundred!

Calling for more men, followed by fewer men,
Seeing his truer men savagely sundered.

Yet did he swing the sword, yet did he face the
   horde
Yet did he act the lord—with his four hundred.

Was there a man dismayed, at these plans
   disarrayed?
While all the cannonade volleyed and thundered?

Theirs not to make reply, theirs not to reason
   why,
Theirs but to ride awry—reckless three hundred!

And as the caucus shrunk, down to a tiny
   chunk
Wasn't the thought bethunk: someone had
   blundered?

Never a thought of it! Not a soul saw to it!
None of them questioned it! Timid two
   hundred . . .

And as the bodies fell, shattered by shot and shell
"What in the bloody hell?" all the land
   wondered.

Yet with endurity, and fullest surity,
Into obscurity rode the one hundred.

And when the smoke had cleared only three men
  appeared
Smiling, though somewhat seared—fortunate trio!

Forward they stiffly rode, bearing their heavy
  load,
Seeking their last abode—Div, Gray, and Theo.

# ANATOMY OF
# BLACK
# CONSCIOUSNESS

*To most white South Africans in mid-1977, Black Consciousness was either nonexistent or a nightmarish manifestation of extremism among blacks that would have to be confronted with force.*

Much is being said these days by white politicians about Black Consciousness, most of it reflecting such abysmal ignorance of the subject that a reply is required.

Those best qualified to reply, the black leaders themselves, are either in prison or banned, so here is yet another white attempt to explain what blacks want in South Africa.

Black Consciousness has its roots in the past. In the 1920s there was a similar movement in South Africa called Garveyism, introduced here by a black American, Marcus Garvey. Garvey was of Caribbean origin, born of parents descended from African slaves.

Garveyism in South Africa had many of the trappings of an American political party, with lapel buttons, but never really caught on throughout the country because black leaders here at the time still hoped to unite with whites in a common society.

This was and remains the policy of the African National Congress, which can be traced back to its inception in 1912.

Then in the late 1950s came the formation of the Pan-Africanist Congress, emphasizing black solidarity, in contrast to the multiracial approach of the ANC.

It was in the late 1960s, however, that Black Consciousness first made its major impact as a reaction to the rigidity of Afrikaner Nationalist determination never to share a common political system with blacks. Young blacks concluded that the black man was on his own, that he couldn't look to whites for unity, and that he must make his very blackness a political weapon.

The beginnings of today's black power sentiment is therefore an inevitable consequence of apartheid. If you spend decades setting people apart because of their skin color they logically strike back on that basis. If you exclude them, they exclude you. If you reject them, they reject you.

But this alone is a simplistic explanation of Black Consciousness, which has more positive aspects than concepts of rejection. It seeks to turn a negative into a positive; to make black people conscious of their worth as people; to offset the centuries of conditioning in South Africa that have given so many blacks as well as so many whites a negative view of blackness.

Black Consciousness seeks to replace such feelings of inferiority and subservience with feelings of confidence based on a sense of black uniqueness. It is intended to make the black man see himself as a being entire in himself rather than an extension of the white world and its concepts.

It is cultural and sociological but above all political, seeing black unity forged out of raised consciousness as a powerful political force. While it emphasizes race, in this sense, as a political strategy, it is not racist in the sense of regarding nonblacks as inferior or to be hated for not being black.

No Black Consciousness spokesperson has ever suggested the exclusion of whites from political processes or social acceptance because of their color, nor is the society they aim at a racially exclusive society.

While they use their blackness as a political weapon to fight the penalties they suffer specifically for being black, and while this process excludes whites as campaign colleagues for the sake of impetus, their ultimate goal is a country in which race is not a factor.

The extent to which they, having led a generation to emphasize its blackness, will be able later to discount such racial consciousness is open to question, but that is seen as a risk whites must run for having made race the issue to begin with.

Black Consciousness devotees are not much concerned with white sensitivities at this stage, considering that their priority is to consider their own sensitivities during their struggle for what they want.

Black Consciousness has certainly created a new breed of young black South African—one who walks tall, looks the world right in the eye, and isn't hesitant about stepping forward to claim rights.

From the ranks of Black Consciousness will come many of South Africa's future leaders, and all South Africans deeply committed to this country should try to understand their thoughts and attitudes.

Like other ticking devices, what makes them tick is explosive in its implications, depending on the white response to Black Consciousness. If that response is understanding and generous, positive progress away from apartheid is possible.

But if the response is negative, relying on the old belief that white power is militarily invincible, there is big trouble looming on the horizon for this country.

# BEHIND
# THE BILTONG
# CURTAIN

*This was written during a week in which South Africa's state-controlled television and radio services were going to extra lengths to depict other countries as having worse problems than South Africa—especially Britain.*

We are so brainwashed on our state-controlled television and radio services that it is necessary to get out of the country occasionally to gain some perspective, especially to visit countries that our propagandists keep assuring us are plunging downhill to disaster.

Like Britain, for instance. Often we are given the impression that Britain is broke, bankrupt, misgoverned, crime-ridden, decadent, shoddy, dull, and unfriendly.

Well, I've just come back from some weeks in Britain,

and you could have fooled me. Rolls-Royces still cruise around London in amazing numbers, the theaters are packed, the concert halls are booked up, opera thrives at Covent Garden, and the London Symphony Orchestra is at its peak of perfection in the Royal Festival Hall.

The natives are as friendly as ever.

Either the Brits are conning us all, or their critics are conning themselves. And that can be unprofitable, as Hitler and Napoleon and others have discovered to their cost.

So if the British are doomed, someone should tell them about it. They obviously don't know.

However, I did read one gloomy editorial in *The Times* of London, deploring the condition of the country, its inept government, its huge economic problems, and its lack of future prospects. It forecast doom and disaster for Britain

It was in a glass case at *The Times* building, and had been written in 1822.

# A CATALOG
# OF WOES

*This was another of those "neutral" articles marking a prudent phase during which it seemed a good idea, in view of government hysteria over criticism, to lie low for a while.*

The eminent barrister Dr. Wilfrid Cooper bought himself a new BMW in Port Elizabeth and set out with happy anticipation to drive it home along the coastal Garden Route to Cape Town.

He was well disposed to give a ride to any hitchhiker likely to ask a barrage of pleasing questions about the treasured new vehicle, and after some miles espied a fellow who had the appearance of one who would appreciate a ride in such a car—the sort of man who would want to know about the horsepower, fuel consumption, performance, and so forth.

But the man simply climbed into the car, stared glumly ahead, and ventured not a word. On closer inspection, furthermore, he seemed less likely to be a connoisseur of automotive excellence. He was unshaven and smelled of liquor.

His mood slightly dashed, Dr. Cooper nevertheless determined to initiate some conversation involving cars and in particular his new car. He asked why the man was hitchhiking. Had he no car of his own?

The man replied that he had once had a car, but that it was now "stukkend," broken. And it was broken because it had been involved in a collision. The other driver was to blame. The other driver had been black. They had collided head-on, and his car had been totally destroyed.

After a long pause he observed that on top of this misfortune he had been sent to prison by Judge Jennett of Grahamstown for three years because of the accident.

Dr. Cooper was shocked at the severity of the sentence for a car accident. Besides, hadn't it been the other driver's fault? Not according to the judge, said the man, adding that the police maintained he had been drunk at the time of the accident.

Still, said Dr. Cooper, who is after all a doctor of law, the sentence seemed heavy for an offense involving no injury.

Well, said the man, his wife and child had been killed in the crash.

After a long pause the man said his wife had been dancing with another man at a party, and so he had driven off very fast with her and the child, and he had had a lot to drink because he wasn't a sissy.

By this time Dr. Cooper's eyes were somewhat glazed over, and to change the subject he asked his passenger the purpose of his journey, upon which the man disclosed that he had been to Port Elizabeth to visit his brother, who had been shot in the brain while up on the borders in military service against "the terrorists."

Dr. Cooper's sympathetic response took the line that the man's parents must be suffering greatly at so much tragedy in the family, whereupon the man said that his father was dead and his mother in prison.

In prison?

Yes, she was serving fifteen years for murdering her boyfriend. The boyfriend, a Mr. Nel, had made her unhappy, and she had poured petrol over him and set him alight and he had died.

Had he visited her in prison? Yes, and she had recently had a breast removed because of cancer.

By now desperate to make the conversation less somber, Dr. Cooper asked the man what he did for a living, and he replied that he was a prison warder but now faced dismissal because a prisoner he was guarding had escaped.

By the time Table Mountain came into view Dr. Cooper was relieved that his passenger asked to be let off in the far suburbs. He had developed the conviction that if this unfortunate man came near enough to the famous mountain, it would collapse onto him.

So if you're ever hitchhiking and a new BMW zooms callously past you it might just be Dr. Wilfrid Cooper choosing a more optimistic view of life.

# A MOST
# UNUSUAL CHILD

*This article dealt with one of the side effects of the Terrorism Act, under which such a wide net was cast that completely innocent persons could be imprisoned and branded as terrorists.*

This week I want you to meet a most unusual child, aged almost four. She is unusual for her age in that she is more withdrawn than most toddlers and is given to breaking her long silences with mature phrases not usually uttered by small children—phrases like: "I want to go to the police station to be arrested."

She doesn't play games like other kids, and adults are often surprised to hear her speaking of things quite unrelated to their conversation, usually about policemen and prisons and arrest.

Yet she comes from a happy home, was brought into the world by loving parents, and from the day of her birth was particularly close to her father, who played with her every evening on his return from work.

The first break in her home life was shortly before her first birthday, when her father was imprisoned without trial under Section 6 of the Terrorism Act and kept for five months in Pretoria Central Prison before being released without explanation or charge.

During this time she became increasingly withdrawn and would often wake up at night crying—something she'd never done before. Her mother bought a record player and some records to cheer her up, but she kept asking when her father was coming home.

In March 1975, when her father was released, she was overjoyed and friends noted the strong bond between the two. Her mother could see a growing physical resemblance between the child and her handsome father.

Then the following year he was again imprisoned without trial, and the child again became obsessed with the police, who had simply come one day and taken her father away for reasons nobody could explain. (Not even the minister of justice.)

Then, last year, her father died in prison while under security police custody. It was alleged that he had hanged himself, but it is strongly doubted whether anyone, including those who made the allegation, believe it.

The child herself refused to believe her father would

never come home again to play with her. Again she grew moody and withdrawn, and again her mother tried vainly to cheer her up.

Early last month things were improving. Her mother had found a typing job and to celebrate she promised the child she would buy some oranges on the way home as a treat.

But she wasn't able to because security police came to her place of work and imprisoned her under the Terrorism Act.

And that is why Motheba Mohapi, not quite four years old, now talks of going to prison so she can be with her parents.

I knew her father and I know her mother. For anyone to suggest either was a "terrorist" is ludicrous. Yet our rulers frequently debase language with words like "terrorist" and "subversive."

If Mapetla Mohapi or his wife, Nohle, were at any stage involved in "terrorism," we may be sure the evidence would gleefully have been presented against them in one of our many political trials.

But until the government actually prosecutes such persons in a proper court of law, their innocence is not only presumed but, in my opinion, proven.

Meanwhile, we may wonder whether such a government has the faintest conception of the hundreds, thousands, millions of black children today sworn to avenge a million wrongs against their parents, whether these wrongs are inflicted through the pass laws, by bulldozing squatter camps and rendering people homeless, or by locking them up and making false accusations against them.

An awful seed is being sown, and we have reason to dread the harvest.

# J'ACCUSE!

*From the date of this article, September 14, 1977, the column changed tone and there were no more jokes. After Steve Biko's death nothing in South Africa seemed amusing.*

I have just received news that my friend Steve Biko has died in detention. He needs no tributes from me, but I have the need to record a deep sense of loss at the death of this extraordinary man, who at the age of thirty had acquired such a towering stature in the minds and hearts of young black people throughout South Africa.

In the three years I knew him my conviction grew that he was the country's most important political leader and certainly the greatest man I ever had the privilege to know. Wisdom, humor, compassion, intellect—he had all these attributes. You could take the most complex problem to him and in one or two sentences he could strike to the core of the matter and provide the obvious solution.

How I wish I could publish for all white South Africans his thoughts about their fears, prejudices, and timidities, and what he saw as the clear answers to these—but the government through its banning orders silenced all his public statements and even in death he may not lawfully be quoted.

He was imprisoned without trial more than once, experiencing solitary confinement several times. He always came out of such ordeals as tough as ever and as humorous about the interrogation sessions. He had a close understanding of his interrogators' fears and motivations and with almost total recall would recount their questions, some of which seemed incredible.

Any contest of wits between him and them was a one-sided mismatch. The only thing that could bring him down was death, and now it has done so.

As to this death, there are enough basic facts known to apportion blame.

The basic facts are that when he was detained about three weeks ago he was fit and healthy; that he was imprisoned without trial; and that he was in the custody of the security police throughout until his death.

Therefore, whatever the cause of his death—I repeat, whatever the cause—I hold responsible all those associated with his detention, because his death occurred while he was under their control, and control exercised through morally wrong powers is morally unjustifiable control, making those who exercise it accountable for all that occurs in terms of it.

And because Minister J. T. Kruger heads the department that exercises such powers, I hold him particularly accountable in this tragedy.

As to those more directly involved in the interrogations to which he was subjected, all things humanly possible will be done to bring their role to light.

Since the death of Steve Biko was announced I have received gloating messages from white racists who rejoice in his death and believe it will aid their cause. They don't realize to what extent his moderation was, preserving the brittle peace in this country.

Now they quote me Old Testament scripture, linking my grief to the creed of retribution.

One might, in the same vein, remind them of an appropriate reply from the New Testament:

"Weep not for me, but for yourselves and for your children."

# DEATH OF
# A GREAT MAN

*It seemed necessary two days later to carry the lament over Steve Biko's death a stage further. It was a time of profound shock and grief.*

I have often written about Steve Biko in this column, in an attempt to acquaint as many South Africans as possible with the special qualities of this remarkable man whose friendship I was privileged to experience for three years.

In a normal society in which he could have written and spoken freely for himself, his unique gifts would have become known to most of his countrymen, but the government edict banning him meant he could not speak publicly or write or be quoted, which meant that whites, at least, knew little or nothing about him.

This was foolish of our rulers, because ultimately they are the main losers thereby. Suppression of moderate leaders only intensifies extreme resistance.

Our rulers think their enemy is words, and that if they prevent certain words being uttered by certain people they have won. But their enemy is thoughts more than words. Words, after all, are merely the reflection of thoughts. The thoughts are what matter, and you cannot legislate against thoughts.

That is why the apartheid policy of our rulers cannot survive indefinitely in South Africa, and why the days of their rule are numbered. The thoughts of too many are against them, and ultimately they themselves are too few.

Yes, Steve Biko has died in detention, and bitter though the grief is in this tragedy, its fruits will be the most bitter for those who might have believed his death would be to their benefit.

Prime Minister Vorster in this country and Prime Minister Smith in Rhodesia thunder out at their party congresses in the names of their countries as if they were Churchills rallying the national ranks in time of crisis. But the difference is that Churchill was rallying a people united in a common aim, whereas Mr. Vorster and Mr. Smith represent ideas massively rejected by most of their compatriots.

Thoughts, again, are responsible. The thoughts that led to apartheid, to racial hostility, to bulldozers demolishing squatter homes, to laws that permit the imprisonment without trial and the death of forty-five dissidents in custody—twenty of them in the past eighteen months.

And these thoughts, in turn, are challenged with opposing thoughts, thoughts of indictment, resentment, bitterness, and hatred.

And a champion of reconciliation and moderation lies dead in detention.

While his death seriously diminishes hopes for the peace he sought for us all, we can only hope his followers will pursue his goal with even stronger purpose.

Will this purpose turn our rulers from their present disastrous course? Are we really headed for the horrors of war in South Africa?

These questions are no longer the living concern of Steve Biko. He has died having done what he could for us.

# QUESTIONS FOR MINISTER KRUGER

*Increasingly the grief over Steve Biko's death was turning to anger, and the most appropriate target for the anger was the politician ultimately responsible for Biko's death.*

Police Minister Kruger has made some strange statements on the death of Steve Biko, and they prompt some specific questions.

First, when told the news of Biko's death, he said: "Biko's death leaves me cold."

He later tried to explain such callousness away by saying he had meant he felt "neutral" about Biko's death.

Then, pressed further, he said: "One feels sorry about any death. I suppose I would feel sorry about my own death."

Then he exchanged quips with a delegate to his party's congress, jocularly agreeing when the delegate commended him for "being so democratic that he gives detainees the democratic right to starve themselves to death."

His first statement on the actual cause of death was that Biko died "following a hunger strike." The clear implication was that Biko starved himself to death.

Now Mr. Kruger has appeared on national television to say that Biko had been fed intravenously.

Mr. Kruger should appear again on national television to answer the following specific questions:

1. Is there a pathological report on the postmortem examination carried out on the body of Steve Biko?
2. Has such a report or any such report been sent to Minister Kruger?
3. If so, what is the substance of this report?
4. If so, does the report support Mr. Kruger's implication that Biko died of malnutrition? Of starvation, in fact?
5. Does Mr. Kruger still stand by his statement about hunger strike?

While he ponders his responses to these questions, it seems appropriate to bring up to date the complete list of persons known to have died in detention under Security Police custody, with the official causes in parentheses.

L. NGUDLE died in Pretoria on September 5, 1963 (suicide by hanging)

B. MERHOPE died in Worcester on September 19, 1963 (causes undisclosed)

J. TYITYA died in Port Elizabeth on January 24, 1964 (suicide by hanging)

S. SALOOJIE died in Johannesburg on September 9, 1964 (fell seven floors during interrogation)

N. GAGA died in Transkei on May 7, 1965 (natural causes)

P. HOYE died in Transkei on May 8, 1965 (natural causes)

J. HAMAKWAYO died in Pretoria in 1966 (suicide by hanging)

H. SHONYEKA died in Pretoria on October 9, 1966 (suicide by hanging)

L. LEONG PIN died in Pretoria on November 19, 1966 (suicide by hanging)

A. AH YAN died in Pretoria on January 5, 1967 (suicide by hanging)

A. MADIBA died in an undisclosed prison on September 9, 1967 (suicide by hanging)

J. TUBAKWE died in Pretoria on September 11, 1968 (suicide by hanging)

AN UNNAMED PERSON died on an unknown day in 1968 (death disclosed under questioning in parliament on January 28, 1969)

N. KGOATHE died in Pretoria on February 4, 1969 (slipped in shower)

S. MODIPANE died in prison on February 28, 1969 (slipped in shower)

J. LENKOE died in Pretoria on March 10, 1969 (suicide by hanging)

C. MAYEKISO died in Port Elizabeth on June 17, 1969 (suicide)

J. MONAKGOTLA died in Pretoria on September 10, 1969 (thrombosis)

IMAM A. HARON died in Cape Town on September 27, 1969 (fell down stairs)

M. CUTHSELA died in undisclosed prison on January 21, 1971 (natural causes)

A. TIMOL died in Johannesburg on October 27, 1971 (leaped from tenth-floor window during interrogation)

J. MDLULI died in Durban on March 19, 1976 (fell against chair during scuffle)

M. MOHAPI died in Kei Road on August 5, 1976 (suicide by hanging)

L. MAZWEMBE died in Cape Town on September 2, 1976 (suicide by hanging)

D. MBATHA died in an undisclosed prison on September 25, 1976 (suicide by hanging)

E. MZOLO died in Johannesburg on October 1, 1976 (no details given)

W. TSHWANE died on October 14, 1976 (no details given)

E. MAMASILA died on November 18, 1976 (no details given)

T. MOSALA died in Butterworth on November 26, 1976 (no details given)

W. TSHAZIBANE died on December 11, 1976 (no details given)

G. BOTHA died in Port Elizabeth on December 14, 1976 (fell down stairwell)

DR. N. NTSHUNTSHA died on January 9, 1977 (no details given)

L. NDZAGA died on January 9, 1977 (no details given)

E. MALEL died on January 20, 1977 (no details given)

M. MABELANE died on February 15, 1977 (no details given)

T. JOYI died on February 15, 1977 (no details given)

S. MALINGA died in Maritzburg on February 22, 1977 (natural causes)

R. KHOZA died in Maritzburg on March 26, 1977 (suicide by hanging)

J. MASHABANE died on June 5, 1977 (suicide)

P. MABIJA died in Kimberley on July 7, 1977 (fell six floors during interrogation)

E. LOZA died in Cape Town on August 1, 1977 (no details given)

DR. H. HAFFEJEE died in Durban on August 3, 1977 (no details given)

B. EMZIZI died on August 5, 1977 (no details given)

F. MOGATUSI died on August 28, 1977 (suffocation in epileptic fit)

S. BIKO died in Pretoria on September 12, 1977 (self-starvation)

Yes, Steve Biko has become the forty-fifth South African to die in security police custody—unaccused, uncharged, unconvicted.

And his is the death they will not be allowed to forget.

This time the whole world is watching them. They will have to have some sort of inquest, and through that process at least some of the truth will emerge.

The name of Steve Biko is going to haunt this government until its last days in South Africa.

# MORE QUESTIONS
# FOR KRUGER

*Kruger had begun to falter in his blustering attempts
to conceal the real cause of Steve Biko's death, and
he went so far as to accuse the dead Biko of having
authored pamphlets urging violence and murder.*

Police Minister Kruger seems
to be losing confidence in his original statement implying that Steve Biko died of self-starvation after a pro-
longed hunger strike.

This is not surprising, because it must by now be clear
even to him that that was not the cause of Biko's death.

This week, accompanied by Steve Biko's widow, I ex-
amined his body in the mortuary in King William's
Town where it had been brought for his burial, and there
was no sign of noticeable loss of weight, let alone malnutrition.

And there are other indications that Mr. Kruger is backing away from his original story—he is now trying to smear the memory of Biko by claiming, as quoted in *Die Burger*, that Biko was found in possession of pamphlets calling for "blood and bodies in the streets" which, Minister Kruger alleges, were written by Biko.

But you only have to read these crude pamphlets to know that Biko couldn't possibly have written them. The grammar is so bad, the English so incorrect, that this man so gifted in syntax and the use of the English language wouldn't even have associated himself with such rubbish.

Any suggestion that Steve Biko wanted violence and bloodshed in this country is a lie—a lie the more despicable and cowardly because it comes after his death when he can't answer back.

Does anyone who knows our security police truly believe that if they had such evidence against Biko they wouldn't have rushed him into court, delighted at last to have something on him?

They would have taken great care to keep him alive and well just for that.

No, these pamphlets, like so many others of that ilk, have been produced by persons weak in English and weaker still in a sense of justice.

One hopes such clumsy efforts to distract public attention from the unanswered questions surrounding Biko's death will be ignored so that Minister Kruger can consider some further questions.

Here they are for him to confirm or deny:

1. Was a sixteen-page pathological report on the post-mortem findings delivered to you last Monday?
2. Does this report indicate that death could have been caused by brain damage consistent with severe impact on the forehead?
3. Does this report mention internal chest injury resulting from impact on the rib cage?
4. Does the report mention any other injuries totally unconnected with hunger-strike theories?

Make another television appearance, Mr. Kruger!

# A KIND
# OF MIRACLE

*The funeral of Steve Biko was such an extraordinary experience that it seemed necessary to describe it to a wide audience, in the hope that its lessons could be absorbed.*

Take a crowd of twenty thousand blacks at the funeral of a well-loved leader who has died while in the custody of white security police; add to their anger more anger at the callousness of Police Minister Kruger for saying such a death leaves him cold; add more anger over police prevention of tens of thousands of other mourners from attending the funeral; and add fresh anger whipped up by emotional speeches against white oppression.

Add to this multitude of angry, grieving blacks a small group of whites intermingled in this huge, volatile crowd, and in this land of racial tension it requires only one stumble, one jostle, one tactless remark to touch off a tragic explosion of retribution.

Yet no incident of the sort took place at the funeral of Steve Biko this week. Through five hours of speeches by spokesmen of all those allegedly anti-white organizations, not one white present was made to feel unwelcome or under direct threat by that emotional multitude.

Not that we few whites were free of fear. Far from it. It was the most frightening five hours of my life. My wife and I were in the middle of the standing crowd and knew many moments of apprehension as the rhetoric was aimed at white viciousness, white cruelty, white exploitation, white privilege, and white murder of black martyrs.

One is very conscious of one's whiteness on such occasions.

Helen Suzman and several other MPs of her party arrived, and blacks on one of the packed stands made way to find a seat for her. But few of the other whites present were well known. Most were young people, and most were surely conscious of the risk they ran.

I think what motivated many of the whites who attended, apart from natural motives of condolence, was an act of faith in the kind of country South Africa could become with apartheid removed and people judged simply as individuals. That certainly was a point made in many of the speeches.

Admittedly it was a minor theme to the major theme of black activism, yet consistent throughout was the message that the end envisaged was a nonracial, non-ethnic society.

That no whites in that crowd were menaced or hurt is a kind of miracle.

Yet if you look at the record, black South Africans are noticeably not racist by inclination. To the extent that one can generalize, they seem not as readily disposed to racial bigotry as so many whites seem to be.

Which, in the circumstances, is also a kind of miracle.

Several whites who had been personal friends of Steve Biko were discernible in the crowd, notably Father David Russell and Dr. Francis Wilson, and all the major embassies were well represented, as were all the major churches.

For my wife and me the greatest sadness on the way home was the realization that the Steve Biko we will miss most painfully is not the revered leader most of the masses will miss, nor the young philosopher the visiting academics will miss, nor the extrovert conversationalist the foreign journalists will miss, but the friend who always made for the same chair in our house, and whose inflections of voice and gesture in lighting a cigarette, quaffing a beer, greeting a child, and slouching for a chat are so vividly remembered.

I think he would say that the reason there were no racial incidents at his funeral was that the people were intermingled, not standing apart in separate racial groups, and that just as hostility grows from separation and isolation, so does love grow from closeness and contact.

The total opposite of apartheid.

# MINISTER KRUGER
# MUST RESIGN!

*Kruger was on the run in his attempt to salvage some credibility. Few believed anything he said about Steve Biko's death, and there were even some signs that his cabinet colleagues were resenting his ineptitude in covering up the facts.*

$S$outh Africa is ruled by fear. This fear breeds hatred, which in turn breeds more fear, in an awful cycle building up towards the explosion of hatred into conflict.

Voices of warning are seen as voices of incitement. Voices of dissidence are labeled as voices of treachery and treason. The peacemakers are being portrayed as the advocates of violence. It has all happened before and it will happen again until prerevolutionary people acquire postrevolutionary wisdom.

South Africa is heading for civil war, escalation of

war along the borders, and increasing hostility from the international community. Yet our government remains intransigent, rejecting peaceful negotiation and opting for military truculence.

If this government really believed its claim that the young whites are solidly with them it wouldn't need conscription. Thousands would be flocking to join the armed forces. But then old politicians have always been ready to send the young to the battlefields.

There are many young white Rhodesians without arms or legs or eyesight today because they followed the folly of Ian Smith in fighting for what the same Ian Smith is now having to negotiate away. Those young men must be wondering now why they made their sacrifice. There would be fewer wars if politicians had to do their own fighting, and there is a special futility in conflict that can be avoided by negotiation, as in our situation.

Peace could be assured in South Africa if the white minority recognized the genuine grievances of the black majority and resolved to come to terms with remedying the gross injustices of apartheid.

But the opposite is happening. Apartheid is on a collision course with black anger as never before and the Afrikaner Nationalists who rule us are underestimating the scale and scope of this anger.

They underestimate it because they are ignorant of the realities of this country, having cut themselves off and crept into a cocoon of such self-preoccupation that they now live in a world of artificial whiteness socially, economically, and politically.

It is a world of parades, medal presentations, and ceremonial exclusivity. They name airports and factories after themselves, congratulate themselves, confer awards on themselves, and forget that the rest of us exist. I fear they are in for a terrible reminder that they are few and the angry blacks are many.

But in their withdrawal into their own limited awareness, our rulers have destroyed much that might have helped them to a realization of their reality. They have done away with most of the liberties reserved to even the few who once had civil rights in this country.

Following the totalitarian path so many of them admire, they have allowed politicians and police to take over the role of judges and jailers, and now they have added Steve Biko to the list of the dead in detention.

It is no longer enough to record and deplore such deaths, and in the case of Biko's death it is certainly not enough to mourn it and deplore it. For me this is one death that marks a turning point and requires appropriate determination to ensure that out of it comes significant advance along the road Steve Biko traveled in search of justice and reconciliation for all South Africans.

The first thing is to nail down the truth about how Steve Biko died.

According to Minister Kruger he died of starvation after a hunger strike.

According to the government's only English-language newspaper, *The Citizen*, he died of nephritis.

Both these claims are untrue, and a postmortem and inquest would show them to be untrue. The true cause of Biko's death will emerge in time, because we, his many friends, will not allow this question to go unanswered.

For South Africa and for this government and for its security police this death is one too many. They have truly gone too far this time.

The price they are going to pay for it is incalculable, and the paying will go on for many years, for as long as it takes to remove this government and every last trace of this policy of apartheid from South Africa.

But first, several things must be done, and we must call for them until they are done:

1. There must be a proper inquest into the death of Steve Biko.
2. The medical findings of the postmortem must be released publicly.
3. Those responsible for his death must be prosecuted.
4. Minister Kruger must resign!

# PUBLISHER'S NOTE

Shortly after the last piece in this book was published, Donald Woods was arrested and taken under security police escort to his home, where he was placed under restriction orders (house arrest) signed by Police Minister Kruger. He was forbidden to write, travel, speak publicly, or be quoted in the press for a period of five years. After his young children's lives were threatened, the author engineered a daring escape from his house in East London, South Africa, to Lesotho. His family, traveling by a different route, met him there. The Woods family was then flown in a small plane across four hundred miles of South African air space to Botswana and ultimately to England.

Following international reaction to Biko's death, pressure from foreign embassies in Pretoria compelled the South African government to order an inquest, at which the presiding magistrate ruled that Biko had died of brain damage caused by severe head injury while in security police custody. No person or persons were held responsible or accountable for the murder.

It was, though, the end of Minister Kruger's career, his cabinet colleagues deciding that his performance had seriously damaged their government's image abroad; he lost his cabinet post, and ultimately, his membership in the governing party.

Today, eleven years later, the Biko killing is still the subject of protests and demonstrations against South African embassies and consulates abroad; the story of the events surrounding Biko's death and Donald Woods's role in exposing the truth about it is the subject of Sir Richard Attenborough's major motion picture, *Cry Freedom*.